LENDING LIBRARY
OLLEGE

KT-445-982

B.C.H.E. – LIBRARY

00028654

NIJINSKY, PAVLOVA, DUNCAN

A DA CAPO PRESS REPRINT SERIES

The Lyric Stage

GENERAL EDITOR: DALE HARRIS
SARAH LAWRENCE COLLEGE

NIJINSKY, PAVLOVA, DUNCAN

Three Lives in Dance
Edited by Paul Magriel

BATH COLLEGE OF HIGHER EDUCATION
SION HILL
LIBRARY
DISCARD

Stock No.	Class No.
770198	792. 84

DA CAPO PRESS · NEW YORK · 1977

Library of Congress Cataloging in Publication Data

Main entry under title:

Nijinsky, Pavlova, Duncan.

(The Lyric stage)
Reprint of 3 works: Nijinsky (1946), Pavlova
(1947), and Isadora Duncan (1947), which were edited
by P. D. Magriel and published by Holt, New York.
1. Nijinsky, Waslaw, 1890-1950. 2. Pavlova,
Anna, 1881-1931. 3. Duncan, Isadora, 1878-1927.
4. Dancers—Biography. I. Magriel, Paul David,
1906-   II. Magriel, Paul David, 1906-   ed.
Nijinsky. 1977. III. Magriel, Paul David,
1906-   ed. Pavlova. 1977. IV. Magriel, Paul
David, 1906-   ed. Isadora Duncan. 1977.
GV1785.A1N54 1977   792.8'092'4 [B]   76-51846
ISBN 0-306-70845-0

This Da Capo Press edition of *Nijinsky, Pavlova, Duncan* combines in
one volume the complete texts and illustrations for three books,
all edited by Paul Magriel originally published in New York during
the years indicated: *Nijinsky: An Illustrated Monograph* (1946);
Pavlova: An Illustrated Monograph (1947); and *Isadora Duncan* (1947).

Published by Da Capo Press, Inc.
A Subsidiary of Plenum Publishing Corporation
227 West 17th Street, New York, N. Y. 10011

All Rights Reserved

Manufactured in the United States of America

NIJINSKY

Portrait. Elliott & Fry, London, 1913.

PREFACE

VASLAV NIJINSKY was the great male dancer of our era. Neither the brevity of his active career, the tragedy of his life, nor the fact that he composed only four ballets has diminished the power of his incredible personality as both dancer and choreographer. The notorious aspects of his madness have enforced his fame, but nothing has lessened his essential greatness and the tremendous fascination and interest he holds for dancers.

The writings on Nijinsky are extensive, and these with his own private diary, edited by his wife, present an exciting and moving mosaic of his life and career. The special material of which this book is composed amplifies the fact and legend of Nijinsky through critical appraisals from the viewpoint of artistic collaborator and professional critic, and perhaps even more spectacularly and accurately through the number of photographs that exist. It is unfortunate that there is no film of Nijinsky dancing, but there are these photographs which span his career from his admission to the Imperial Ballet School in Russia to the melancholy days in Swiss confinement. It is from these that there emerges a vast evidence of his extraordinary theatrical style, his peculiar and complete talent for spiritual identification with his roles, and his wonderful comprehension of balletic elegance and deportment.

This book is the first of a series of illustrated monographs on the great dancers of our time which will include, in the near future, studies of Pavlova and Isadora Duncan. Like the present volume they will consist of special essays on various aspects of their lives and careers. Also like the present work there will be a full pictorial record and a bibliography.

CONTENTS

ACKNOWLEDGMENTS

THE major part of the material in this book was made available through the courtesy of *Dance Index* which I acknowledge with thanks for the following:

"The Russian Ballet and Nijinsky." Carl Van Vechten. (Reprinted from his *Interpreters*, Alfred A. Knopf, New York, 1916.)

"Notes on Nijinsky Photographs." Edwin Denby.

"Nijinsky and Til Eulenspiegel." Robert Edmond Jones.

"The Strangeness of Til." H. T. Parker. (First appeared in the Boston *Transcript*, 1916.)

"The Drawings of Nijinsky" by Marsden Hartley is an extract from an unpublished manuscript in the Museum of Modern Art and was made available through the courtesy of Norma Berger of the Marsden Hartley estate. Thanks are due also to the Museum of Modern Art for the photograph of the Bakst portrait and to the Kamin Dance Bookshop for the loan of the photograph of Nijinsky and his wife in their car. For other courtesies I wish to thank the Music Division, New York Public Library, Mr. George Amberg of the Dance and Theater department, Museum of Modern Art, and Mr. David Mann for the use of the photographs of Zobeide.

P. M.

N I J I N S K Y

THE RUSSIAN BALLET
AND NIJINSKY

BY CARL VAN VECHTEN

SERGEI DIAGHILEV brought the dregs of the Russian Ballet to New York and, after a first greedy gulp, inspired by curiosity to get a taste of this highly advertised beverage, the public drank none too greedily. The scenery and the costumes, designed by Bakst, Roerich, Benois, and Larionov, and the music by Rimsky-Korsakov, Tcherepnine, Schumann, Borodin, Balakirev, and Stravinsky—especially Stravinsky—arrived. It was to be deplored, however, that Bakst had seen fit to replace the original décor of *Scheherazade* by a new setting in rawer colors, in which the flaming orange fairly burned into the ultramarine and green (readers of *A Rebours* will remember that des Esseintes designed a room something like this). A few of the dancers came, but of the best not a single one. Nor was Fokine, the dancer-producer, who devised the choreography for *The Firebird*, *Cléopâtre*, and *Petrouchka*, among the number, although his presence had been announced and expected. To those enthusiasts—and they included practically everyone who had seen the Ballet in its greater glory—who had prepared their friends for an overwhelmingly brilliant spectacle, overusing the phrase "a perfect union of the arts," the early performances in January, 1916, at the Century Theatre were a great disappointment. Often had we urged that the individual played but a small part in this new and gorgeous entertainment, but now we were forced to admit that the ultimate glamour was lacking in the ensemble, which was obviously no longer the glad, gay entity it once had been.

The picture was still there, the music (not always too well played), but the interpretation was mediocre. The agile Massine could scarcely be called either a great dancer or a great mime. He had been chosen by Diaghilev for the role of Joseph in Richard Strauss's version of the Potiphar legend but, during the course of a London season carried through without the co-operation of Nijinsky, this was the only part allotted to him. In New York he inter-

1

preted, not without humor and with some technical skill, the incidental divertissement from Rimsky-Korsakov's opera, *The Snow Maiden*, against a vivid background by Larionov. The uninspired choreography of this ballet was also ascribed to Massine by the program, although probably in no comminatory spirit. In the small role of Eusebius in *Carnaval* and in the negligible part of the Prince in *The Firebird* he was entirely satisfactory, but it was impertinent of the Direction to assume that he would prove an adequate substitute for Nijinsky in roles to which that dancer had formerly applied his extremely finished art.

Adolph Bolm contributed his portraits of the Moor in *Petrouchka*, of Pierrot in *Carnaval*, and of the Chief Warrior in the dances from *Prince Igor*. These three roles completely express the possibilities of Bolm as a dancer or an actor, and sharply define his limitations. His other parts, Darkon in *Daphnis et Chloë*, Sadko, the Prince in *Thamar*, Amoun in *Cléopâtre*, the Slave in *Scheherazade*, and Pierrot in *Papillons*, are only variations on the three afore-mentioned themes. His friends often confuse his vitality and abundant energy with a sense of characterization and a skill as a dancer which he does not possess. For the most part he is content to express himself by stamping his heels and gnashing his teeth, and when, as in *Cléopâtre*, he attempts to convey a more subtle meaning to his general gesture, he is not very successful. Bolm is an interesting and useful member of the organization, but he could not make or unmake a season; nor could Gavrilov, who is really a fine dancer in his limited way, although he is unfortunately lacking in magnetism or any power of characterization.

But it was on the distaff side of the cast that the Ballet seemed pitifully undistinguished, even to those who did not remember the early Paris seasons when the roster included the names of Anna Pavlova, Tamara Karsavina, Katerina Geltzer, and Ida Rubinstein. The leading feminine dancer of the troupe when it gave its first exhibitions in New York was Xenia Maclezova, who had not, so far as my memory serves, danced in any London or Paris season of the Ballet (except for one gala performance at the Paris Opéra which pre-ceded the American tour) unless in some very menial capacity. This dancer, like so many others, had the technique of her art at her toes' ends. Sarah Bernhardt once told a reporter that the acquirement of technique never did any harm to an artist, and if one were not an artist it was not a bad thing to have. I have forgotten how many times Mlle. Maclezova could *pirouette* without touching the toe in the air to the floor, but it was some prodigious number. She was past mistress of the *entrechat* and other mysteries of the ballet academy. Here, however, her knowledge of her art seemed to end, in the subjugation of its very mechanism. She was very nearly lacking in those qualities of grace, poetry, and imagination with which great artists are freely endowed, and although she could not actually have been a woman of more than average weight, she often conveyed to the spectator an impression of heaviness. In such a work as *The Firebird*, she really offended the eye. Far from interpreting the ballet, she gave you an idea of how it should not be done.

Her season with the Russians was terminated in very short order, and Lydia Lopoukova, who happened to be in America, and who, indeed, had already been engaged for certain roles, was rushed into her vacant slippers. Now, Mme. Lopoukova had charm as a dancer, whatever her deficiencies in technique. In certain parts, notably as Colombine in *Carnaval*, she assumed a roguish demeanor which was very fetching. As La Ballerine in *Petrouchka*, too, she met all the requirements of the action. But in *Le Spectre de la Rose*, *Les Sylphides*, *The Firebird*, and *La Princesse Enchantée*,* she floundered hopelessly out of her element.

Tchernicheva, one of the lesser but more steadfast luminaries of the Ballet, in the roles for which she was cast, the principal Nymph in *L'Après-midi d'un Faune*, Echo in *Narcisse*, and the Princess in *The Firebird*, more than fulfilled her obligations to the ensemble, but her opportunities in these mimic plays were not of sufficient importance to enable her to carry the brunt of the performances on her lovely shoulders. Flore Revalles was drafted, I understand, from a French opera company. I have been told that she sings—Tosca is one of her roles—as well as she dances. That may very well be. To impressionable spectators she seemed a real *femme fatale*. Her Cléopâtre suggested to me a Parisian cocotte much more than an Egyptian queen. It would be blasphemy to compare her with Ida Rubinstein in this role—Ida Rubinstein, who was true Aubrey Beardsley! In Thamar and Zobeide, both to a great extent dancing roles, Mlle. Revalles, both as dancer and actress, was but a frail substitute for Karsavina.

The remainder of the company was adequate, but not large, and the ensemble was by no means so brilliant as those who had seen the Ballet in London or Paris might have expected. Nor in the absence of Fokine, that master of detail, were performances sufficiently rehearsed. There was, of course, explanation in plenty for this disintegration. Gradually, indeed, the Ballet as it had existed in Europe had suffered a change. Only a miracle and a fortune combined would have sufficed to hold the original company intact. It was not held intact, and the war made further inroads on its integrity. Then for the trip to America many of the dancers probably were inclined to demand double pay. Undoubtedly, Sergei Diaghilev had many more troubles than those which were celebrated in the public prints, and it must be admitted that, even with his weaker company, he gave us finer exhibitions of stage art than had previously been even the exception here.

* This was the name given that season to the Bluebird Variation from *The Sleeping Beauty*.

3

Nijinsky in *Les Sylphides.*

In the circumstances, however, certain pieces, which were originally produced when the company was in the flush of its first glory, should never have been presented here at all. It was not the part of reason, for example, to pitchfork on the Century stage an indifferent performance of *Le Pavillon d'Armide*, in which Nijinsky once disported himself as the favorite slave, and which, as a matter of fact, requires a company of virtuosi to make it a passable diversion. *Cléopâtre*, in its original form, with Nijinsky, Fokine, Pavlova, Ida Rubinstein, and others, hit all who saw it square between the eyes. The absurdly expurgated edition, with its inadequate cast, offered to New York was but the palest shadow of the sensuous entertainment that had aroused all Paris, from the Batignolles to the Bastille. The music, the setting, the costumes—what else was left to celebrate? The altered choreography, the deplorable interpretation, drew tears of rage from at least one pair of eyes. It was quite incomprehensible also why *The Firebird*, which depended on the grace and poetical imagination of the filmiest and most fairylike actress-dancer, should have found a place in the repertoire. It is the dancing equivalent of a coloratura soprano role in opera. Thankful, however, for the great joy of having reheard Stravinsky's wonderful score, I am willing to overlook this tactical error.

All things considered, it is small wonder that a large slice of the paying population of New York tired of the Ballet in short order. One reason for this cessation of interest was the constant repetition of ballets. In London and Paris the seasons as a rule have been shorter, and on certain evenings of the week opera has taken the place of the dance. It has been rare indeed that a single work has been repeated more than three or four times during an engagement. I have not found it stupid to listen to and look at perhaps fifteen performances of varying degrees of merit of *Petrouchka*, *Scheherazade*, *Carnaval*, and the dances from *Prince Igor;* I would rather see the Russian Ballet repeatedly, even as it existed in America, than four thousand five hundred and six Broadway plays or seventy-three operas at the Metropolitan once, but I dare say I may look upon myself as an exception.

At any rate, when the company entered upon a four weeks' engagement at the Metropolitan Opera House, included in the regular subscription season of opera, the subscribers groaned; many of them groaned aloud, and wrote letters to the management and to the newspapers. To be sure, during the tour which had followed the engagement at the Century the repertoire had been increased, but the company remained the same—until the coming of Waslaw Nijinsky.

When America was first notified of the impending visit of the Russian Ballet it was also promised that Waslaw Nijinsky and Tamara Karsavina would head the organization. It was no fault of the American direction or of Sergei Diaghilev that they did not do so. Various excuses were advanced for the failure of Karsavina to forsake her family in Russia and to undertake the journey to the United States, but whatever the cause, there seems to remain no doubt that she refused to come. As for Nijinsky, he, with his wife, had been a prisoner in an Austrian detention camp since the beginning of the war. Wheels were set grinding, but wheels grind slowly in an epoch of international bloodshed, and it was not until March, 1916, that the Austrian ambassador at Washington was able to announce that Nijinsky had been set free.

I do not believe the coming to this country of any other celebrated person had been more widely advertised, although P. T. Barnum may have gone further in describing the charitable and vocal qualities of Jenny Lind. Nijinsky had been extravagantly praised, not only by the official press representatives but also by eminent critics and private persons, in adjectives which seemed to preclude any possibility of his living up to them. I myself had been among the paean singers. I had thrust "half-man, half-god" into print. "A flame!" cried someone. Another, "A jet of water from a fountain!" Such men in the street as had taken the trouble to consider the subject at all very likely expected the arrival of some stupendous and immortal monstrosity, a gravity-defying being with sixteen feet (at least), who bounded like a rubber ball, never touching the solid stage except at the beginning and end of the evening's performance.

Nijinsky arrived in April. Almost immediately he gave vent to one of those expressions of temperament often associated with interpretative genius, the kind of thing I have described at some length in *Music and Bad Manners*. He was not all pleased with the Ballet as he found it. Interviewed, he expressed his displeasure in the newspapers. The managers of the organization wisely remained silent, and a controversy was avoided, but the public had received a suggestion of petulance which could not contribute to the popularity of the new dancer.

Nijinsky danced for the first time in New York on the afternoon of April 12, at the Metropolitan Opera House. The pieces in which he appeared that day were *Le Spectre de la Rose* and *Petrouchka*. Some of us feared that eighteen months in a detention camp would have stamped their mark on the dancer. As a matter of fact, his connection with the Russian Ballet had been severed in 1913, a year before the war began. I can say for myself that on the occasion of his first appearance in America I was probably a good deal more nervous than Nijinsky. It would have been a cruel disappointment to me to discover that his art had deteriorated during the intervening years since I had last seen him. My fears were soon dissipated. A few seconds after he, as the Rose Ghost, had bounded through the window, it was evident that he was in possession of all his powers; nay, more, that he had added to the refinement and polish of his style. I had called Nijinsky's dancing perfection in years gone by, because it so far surpassed that of his nearest rival; now he had surpassed himself. True artists, indeed, have a habit of accomplishing this feat. I may call to your attention the careers of Olive Fremstad, Yvette Guilbert, and Marie Tempest. Later I learned that this first impression might be relied on. Nijinsky, in sooth, has now no rivals upon the stage. One can only compare him with himself.

The Weber-Gautier dance-poem, from the very beginning until the end, when he leaps out of the girl's chamber into the night, affords this great actor-dancer one of his most grateful opportunities. It is in this very part, perhaps, which requires almost unceasing exertion for nearly twelve minutes, that Nijinsky's powers of co-ordination, mental, imaginative, muscular, are best displayed. His dancing is accomplished in that flowing line, without a break between poses and gestures, which is the despair of all novices and almost all other virtuosi. After a particularly difficult leap or toss of the legs or arms, it is a marvel to observe how, without an instant's pause to regain his poise, he rhythmically glides into the succeeding gesture. His dancing has the unbroken quality of music, the balance of great painting, the meaning of fine literature, and the emotion inherent in all these arts. There is something of transmutation in his performances; he becomes an alembic, transforming movement into a finely wrought and beautiful work of art. The dancing of Nijinsky is first an imaginative triumph, and the spectator, perhaps, should not be interested in further dissection of it, but a more intimate observer must realize that behind this the effect produced depends on his supreme command of his muscles. It is not alone the final informing and magnetized imaginative quality that most other dancers lack; it is also just this muscular co-ordination. Observe Gavrilov in the piece under discussion, in which he gives a good imitation of Nijinsky's general style, and you will see that he is unable to maintain this rhythmic continuity.

Nijinsky's achievements become all the more remarkable when one remembers that he is working with an imperfect physical medium. Away from the scene he is an insignificant figure, short and ineffective in appearance. Aside from the pert expression of his eyes, he is like a dozen other young Russians. Put him unintroduced into a drawing room with Jacques Copeau, Orchidée, Doris Keane, Bill Haywood, the Baroness de Meyer, Paulet Thévenaz, the Marchesa Casati, Marcel Duchamp, Cathleen Nesbitt, H. G. Wells, Anna Pavlova, Rudyard Chennevière, Vladimir Rebikov, Henrie Waste, and Isadora Duncan,

Nijinsky in *Le Spectre de la Rose*. De Meyer, Paris, 1911.

and he probably would pass entirely unnoticed. On the stage it may be observed that the muscles of his legs are overdeveloped and his ankles are too large; that is, if you are in the mood for picking flaws, which most of us are not in the presence of Nijinsky in action. Here, however, stricture halts confounded; his head is set on his shoulders in a manner to give satisfaction to a great sculptor, and his torso, with its slender waistline, is quite beautiful. On the stage, Nijinsky makes of himself what he will. He can look tall or short, magnificent or ugly, fascinating or repulsive. Like all great interpretative artists, he remolds himself for his public appearances. It is under the electric light in front of the painted canvas that he becomes a personality, and that personality is governed only by the scenario of the ballet he is representing.

From the day of Nijinsky's arrival, the ensemble of the ballet improved; somewhat of the spontaneity of the European performances was regained; a good deal of the glamour was recaptured; the loose lines were gathered taut, and the choreography of Fokine (Nijinsky is a director as well as a dancer) was restored to some of its former power. He appeared in nine roles in New York during the two short seasons in which he was seen with the Russian Ballet here; the Slave in *Scheherazade*, Petrouchka, the Rose Ghost, the Faun, the Harlequin in *Carnaval*, Narcisse, Til Eulenspiegel, and the principal male roles of *La Princesse Enchantée* and *Les Sylphides*. To enjoy the art of Nijinsky completely, to fully appreciate his genius, it is necessary not only to see him in a variety of parts, but also to see him in the same role many times.

Study the detail of his performance in *Scheherazade*, for example. Its precision alone is noteworthy. Indeed, precision is a quality we see exposed so seldom in the theater that when we find it we are almost inclined to hail it as genius. The role of the Slave in this ballet is perhaps Nijinsky's scenic masterpiece—exotic eroticism expressed in so high a key that its very existence seems incredible on our puritanic stage, and yet with such great art (the artist always expresses himself with beauty) that the intention is softened by the execution. Before the arrival of this dancer, *Scheherazade* had become a police-court scandal. There had been talk of a "Jim Crow" performance in which the blacks were to be separated from the whites in the harem, and I am told that our provincial police magistrates even wished to replace the "mattresses"—so were the divans of the sultanas described in court— by rocking chairs! But to the considerably more vivid *Scheherazade* of Nijinsky no exception was taken. This strange, curious, head-wagging, simian creature, scarce human, wriggled through the play, leaving a long streak of lust and terror in his wake. Never did Nijinsky as the Negro Slave touch the Sultana, but his subtle and sensuous fingers fluttered close to her flesh, clinging once or twice questioningly to a depending tassel. Pierced by the javelins of the Sultan's men, the Slave's death struggle might have been revolting and gruesome. Instead Nijinsky carried the eye rapidly upward with his tapering feet as they balanced for the briefest part of a second straight high in the air, only to fall inert with so brilliantly swift a movement that the aesthetic effect grappled successfully with the feeling of disgust which might have been aroused. This was acting, this was characterization, so completely merged in rhythm that the result became a perfect whole and not a combination of several intentions, as so often results from the work of an actor-dancer.

The heartbreaking Petrouchka, the roguish Harlequin, the Chopiniac of *Les Sylphides*— all were offered to our view; and *Narcisse*, in which Nijinsky not only did some very beautiful dancing, but posed (as the Greek youth admired himself in the mirror of the pool) with such utter and arresting grace that even here he awakened a new kind of emotion. In *La Princesse Enchantée* he merely danced, but how he danced! Do you who saw him still remember those flickering fingers and toes? "He winketh with his eyes, he speaketh with his feet, he teacheth with his fingers," is written in the Book of Proverbs, and the writer might have had in mind Nijinsky in *La Princesse Enchantée*. All these parts were differentiated, all completely realized, in the threefold intricacy of this baffling art, which perhaps is not an art at all until it is so realized, when its plastic, rhythmic, and histrionic elements become an entity.

After a summer in Spain and Switzerland without Nijinsky, the Russian Ballet returned to America for a second season, opening at the Manhattan Opera House, October 16, 1916. It is always a delight to hear and see performances in this theater, and it was found that the brilliance of the Ballet was much enhanced by its new frame. The season, however, opened with a disappointment. It had been announced that Nijinsky would dance on the first night his choreographic version of Richard Strauss's tone-poem, *Til Eulenspiegel*. It is not the first time that a press agent has made a false prophecy. While rehearsing the new work, Nijinsky twisted his ankle, and during the first week of the engagement he did not appear at all. This was doubly unfortunate, because the company was weaker than it had been the previous season, lacking both Massine and Tchernicheva. The only novelty (for America) produced during the first week was an arrangement of the divertissement from Rimsky-Korsakov's opera, *Sadko*, which had already been given a few times in Paris and London by the Ballet, never with conspicuous success. The second week of the season, Nijinsky returned to appear in three roles, the Faun, Til Eulenspiegel, and the Slave in

Scheherazade. Of his performance to Debussy's lovely music I have written elsewhere; nor did this new vision cause me to revise my opinions.

Til Eulenspiegel is the only new ballet the Russians have produced in America. (*Soleil de Nuil* was prepared in Europe, and performed once at the Paris Opéra before it was seen in New York. Besides, it was an arrangement of dances from an opera which is frequently given in Russia and which has been presented at the Opéra-Comique in Paris.) The *chef d'orchestre*, Pierre Monteux, refused to direct performances of this work, on the ground that the composer was not only a German, but a very much alive and active German patriot. On the occasions, therefore, that *Til* was performed in New York, the orchestra struggled along under the baton of Dr. Anselm Goetzl. In selecting this work and in his arrangement of the action Nijinsky was moved, no doubt, by consideration for the limitations of the company as it existed. The scenery and costumes by Robert E. Jones, of New York, were decidedly diverting—the best work this talented young man has done, I think. Over a deep, spreading background of ultramarine, the crazy turrets of medieval castles leaned dizzily to and fro. The costumes were exaggerations of the exaggerated fashions of the Middle Ages. Mr. Jones added feet of stature to the already elongated peaked headdresses of the period. The trains of the velvet robes, which might have extended three yards, were allowed to trail the full depth of the Manhattan Opera House stage. The colors were oranges, reds, greens, and blues, those indeed of Bakst's *Scheherazade*, but so differently disposed that they made an entirely dissimilar impression. The effect reminded one spectator of a Spanish omelet.

In arranging the scenario, Nijinsky followed in almost every detail Wilhelm Klatte's description of the meaning of the music, which is printed in program books whenever the tone-poem is performed, without Strauss's authority, but sometimes with his sanction. Nijinsky was quite justified in altering the end of the work, which hangs the rogue-hero, into another practical joke. His version of this episode fits the music and, in the original Til Eulenspiegel stories, Til is not hanged, but dies in bed. The keynote of Nijinsky's interpretation was gaiety. He was as utterly picaresque as the work itself; he reincarnated the spirit of Gil Blas; indeed, a new quality crept into stage expression through this characterization. Margaret Wycherly, one of the most active admirers of the dancer, told me after the first performance that she felt that he had for the first time leaped into the hearts of the great American public, whose appreciation of his subtler art as expressed in *Narcisse*, *Petrouchka*, and even *Scheherazade*, had been more moderate. There were those who protested that this was not the Til of the German legends, but any actor who attempts to give form to a folk or historical character, or even a character derived from fiction, is forced to run counter to many an observer's preconceived ideas.

"It is an error to believe that pantomime is merely a way of doing without words," writes Arthur Symons, "that it is merely the equivalent of words. Pantomime is thinking overheard. It begins and ends before words have formed themselves, in a deeper consciousness than that of speech. And it addresses itself, by the artful limitations of its craft, to universal human experience, knowing that the moment it departs from those broad lines it will become unintelligible. It risks existence on its own perfection, as the rope-dancer does, to whom a false step means a downfall. And it appeals democratically to people of all nations. . . . And pantomime has that mystery which is one of the requirements of true art. To watch it is like dreaming. How silently, in dreams, one gathers the unheard sounds of words from the lips that do but make pretense of saying them! And does not everyone know that terrifying impossibility of speaking which fastens one to the ground for the eternity of a second, in what is the new, perhaps truer, computation of time in dreams? Something like that sense of suspense seems to hang over the silent actors in pantomime, giving them a nervous exaltation, which has its subtle, immediate effect upon us, in tragic and comic situation. The silence becomes an atmosphere, and with a very curious power of giving distinction to form and motion. I do not see why people should ever break silence on the stage except to speak poetry. Here, in pantomime, you have a gracious, expressive silence, beauty of gesture, a perfectly discreet appeal to the emotions, a transposition of the world into an elegant accepted convention."

Arthur Symons wrote these words before he had seen the Russian Ballet, before the Russian Ballet, as we know it, existed; indeed, before Nijinsky had begun to dance in public, and he felt that the addition of poetry and music to pantomime—the Wagner music-drama, in other words—brought about a perfect combination of the arts. Nevertheless, there is an obvious application of his remarks to the present instance. There is, indeed, the quality of a dream about the characters Nijinsky presents to us. I remember once, at a performance of the Russian Ballet, I sat in a box next to a most intelligent man, a writer himself; I was meeting him for the first time, and he was seeing the ballet for the first time. Before the curtain rose he had told me that dancing and pantomime were very pretty to look at, but that he found no stimulation in watching them, no mental and spiritual exaltation, such as might follow a performance of *Hamlet*. Having seen Nijinsky, I could not agree with him—and this indifferent observer became that evening himself a fervent disciple of the Ballet. For Nijinsky gave him, he found, just what his ideal performance of Shakespeare's play might have given him, a basis for dreams, for thinking, for poetry. The ennobling effect of all great and perfect art, after the primary emotion, seems to be to set our minds wandering in a thousand channels, to suggest new outlets. Pater's experience before the *Mona Lisa* is unique only in its intense and direct expression.

No writer, no musician, no painter, can feel deep emotion before a work of art without expressing it in some way, although the expression may be a thousand leagues removed from the inspiration. And how few of us can view the art of Nijinsky without emotion! To the painter he gives a new sense of proportion, to the musician a new sense of rhythm, while to the writer he must perforce immediately suggest new words; better still, new meanings for old words. Dance, pantomime, acting, harmony, all these divest themselves of their worn-out accoutrements and appear, as if clothed by magic, in garments of un-heard-of novelty; hue, texture, cut, and workmanship are all a surprise to us. We look enraptured, we go away enthralled, and perhaps even unconsciously a new quality creeps into our own work. It is the same glamour cast over us by contemplation of the Campo Santo at Pisa, or the Roman Theatre at Orange, or the Cathedral at Chartres—the inspiration for one of the most word-jeweled books in any language—or the New York sky line at twilight as one sails away into the harbor, or a great iron crane which lifts tons of alien matter in its gaping jaw. Great music can give us this feeling, the symphonies of Beethoven, Mozart's *Don Giovanni*, Schubert's C major symphony, or César Franck's D minor, *The Sacrifice to the Spring* of Stravinsky, *L'Après-midi d'un Faune* of Debussy, Chabrier's Rhapsody, *España;* great interpretative musicians can give it to us, Ysaye at his best, Paderewski, Marcella Sembrich in song recital; but how few artists on the stage suggest even as much as the often paltry lines of the author, the often banal music of the composer! There is an *au delà* to all great interpretative art, something that remains after story, words, picture, and gesture have faded vaguely into that storeroom in our memories where are concealed these lovely ghosts of ephemeral beauty, and the artist who is able to give us this is blessed even beyond his knowledge, for to him has been vouchsafed the sacred kiss of the gods. This quality cannot be acquired; it cannot even be described; but it can be felt. With its beneficent aid the interpreter not only contributes to our pleasure, he broadens our horizon, adds to our knowledge and capacity for feeling.

As I read over these notes I realize that I have not been able to discover flaws in the art of this young man. It seems to me that in his chosen medium he approaches perfection. What he attempts to do, he always does perfectly. Can one say as much for any other interpreter? But it is a difficult matter to give the spirit of Nijinsky, to describe his art on paper, to capture in ink the abundant grace, the measureless poetry, the infinite illusion of his captivating motion. Who can hope to do it? Future generations must take our word for his greatness. We can do little more than call it that. I shall have served my purpose if I have succeeded in this humble article in bringing back to those who have seen him a flashing glimpse of the imaginative actuality.

Nijinsky in *Petrouchka*. Elliott & Fry, London, 1911.

NOTES ON
NIJINSKY PHOTOGRAPHS

BY EDWIN DENBY

LOOKING at the photographs of Nijinsky, one is struck by his expressive neck. It is an unusually thick and long neck. But its expressivity lies in its clear lift from the trunk, like a powerful thrust. The shoulders are not square, but slope downward; and so they leave the neck easily free, and the eye follows their silhouette down the arms with the sense of a line extraordinarily extended into space, as in a picture by Cézanne or Raphael. The head therefore, at the other end of this unusual extension, poised up in the air, gains an astonishing distinctness, and the tilt of it, even with no muscular accentuation, becomes of unusual interest. Nijinsky tilts his head lightly from the topmost joint, keeping this joint mobile 'against the upright thrust of the other vertebrae. He does not bend the neck back as some contemporary ballet dancers do. Seen from the side or the rear, the upward line of his back continues straight into the uprightness of the neck, like the neck of a Maillol statue. But Nijinsky alters his neck to suit a character role. The change is striking in the *Scheherazade* pictures—and Mr. Van Vechten, who saw him dance the part, describes him as a "head-wagging, simian creature." Another variation is that for *Petrouchka*, where the shoulders are raised square to break the continuity of the silhouette; to make the arms dangle as a separate entity, and make the head independently wobbly as a puppet's is, on no neck to speak of. The head here does not sum up or direct the action of the body; it seems to have only a minor, a pathetic function. But it bobs too nonsensically to be humanly pitiful. In the role of the Faun the shoulders are slightly lifted when the Faun becomes dimly aware of his own emotion; but the neck is held up firmly and candidly against the shoulder movement (which would normally press the neck to a forward slant); and so the silhouette is kept self-contained and the figure keeps its dignity. Notice, too, the neck in the reclining position of the Faun. Another poignant duplicity of emotion is expressed by

15

the head, neck, and shoulder line of the *Jeux* photographs—the neck rising against lifted shoulders and also bent sideways against a counter tilt of the head. The hero in *Jeux* seems to meet pathos with human nobility; not as the Faun does, with animal dignity.

Looking in these photographs farther along the figure, at the arms in particular, one is struck by their lightness, by the way in which they seem to be suspended in space. Especially in the pictures from *Pavillon* and from *Spectre*, they are not so much placed correctly, or advantageously or illustratively; rather they seem to flow out unconsciously from the moving trunk, a part of the fullness of its intention. They are pivoted, not lifted, from the shoulder or shoulder blade; their force—like the neck's—comes from the full strength of the back. And so they lead the eye more strongly back to the trunk than out beyond their reach into space. Even when they point, one is conscious of the force pointing quite as much as the object pointed at. To make a grammatical metaphor, the relation of subject to object is kept clear. This is not so simple in movement as a layman might think. A similar clarification of subject and object struck me in the bullfighting of Belmonte. His own body was constantly the subject of his motions, the bull the object. With other fighters, one often had the impression that not they personally, but their cloth was the subject that determined the fight. As a cloth is a dead thing, it can only be decorative, and the bull edged into the position of the subject; and the distinctness of the torero's drama was blurred. Nijinsky gives an effect in his arm gesture of himself remaining at the center of space, a strength of voluntary limitation related, in a way, to that of Spanish dance gesture.—This is what makes a dancer's arms look like a man's instead of a boy's.

An actual "object" to a dancer's "subject" is his partner. In dancing with a partner there is a difference between self-effacement and courtesy. Nijinsky in his pictures is a model of courtesy. The firmness of support he gives his partner is complete. He stands straight enough for two. His expression toward her is intense—in *Giselle* it expresses a supernatural relation, in *Pavillon* one of admiration, in *Faune* one of desire, in *Spectre* one of tenderness—and what a supporting arm that is in *Spectre*, as long and as strong as two. But he observes as well an exact personal remoteness, he shows clearly the fact that they are separate bodies. He makes a drama of their nearness in space. And in his own choreography—in *Faune*—the space between the figures becomes a firm body of air, a lucid statement of relationship, in the way intervening space does in the modern academy of Cézanne, Seurat, and Picasso.

One is struck by the massiveness of his arms. This quality also leads the eye back to the trunk, as in a Michelangelo figure. But it further gives to their graceful poses an amplitude of strength that keeps them from looking innocuous or decorative. In particular in the Narcissus pose the savage force of the arms and legs makes credible that the hero's narcism was not vanity, but an instinct that killed him, like an act of God. In the case of *Spectre*, the power of the arms makes their tendrillike bendings as natural as curvings are in a powerful world of young desire; while weaker and more charming arms might suggest an effeminate or saccharine coyness. There is indeed nothing effeminate in these gestures; there is far too much force in them.

It is interesting to try one's self to assume the poses on the pictures, beginning with arms, shoulders, neck, and head. The flowing line they have is deceptive. It is an unbelievable strain to hold them. The plastic relationships turn out to be extremely complex. As the painter de Kooning, who knows the photographs well and many of whose ideas I am using in these notes, remarked: Nijinsky does just the opposite of what the body would naturally do. The plastic sense is similar to that of Michelangelo and Raphael. One might say that the grace of them is not derived from avoiding strain, as a layman might think, but from the heightened intelligibility of the plastic relations. It is an instinct for countermovement so rich and so fully expressed, it is unique; though the plastic theory of countermovement is inherent in ballet technique.

Nijinsky's plastic vitality animates the poses derived from dances by Petipa or Fokine. It shines out, too, if one compares his pictures with those of other dancers in the same parts. This aspect of his genius appears to me one basis for his choreographic style, which specifies sharply plastic effects in dancing—and which in this sense is related both to Isadora and to the moderns. Unfortunately the dancers who now take the role of the Faun do not have sufficient plastic discipline to make clear the intentions of the dance.

From the photographs one can see that the present dancers of *Faune* have not even learned Nijinsky's stance. Nijinsky not only squares his shoulders far less, but also frequently not at all. He does not pull in his stomach and lift his thorax. Neither in shoulders nor chest does he exhibit his figure. His stomach has more expression than his chest. In fact, looking at his trunk, one notices a similar tendency to flat-chestedness (I mean in the stance, not in the anatomy) in all the pictures. It is, I believe, a Petersburg trait, and shared independently by Isadora and Martha Graham. In these photographs, at any rate, the expression does not come from the chest; it comes from below the chest, and flows up through it from below. The thorax, so to speak, passively, is not only pulled at the top up and back; at the bottom and from the side it is also pulled down and back. Its physical function is that of completing the circuit of muscles that hold the pelvis in relation to the spine. And it is this relation that gives the dancer his balance. Balance (or aplomb, in ballet) is the crux of technique. If you want to see how good a dancer is, look at his stomach. If he is sure of himself there, if he is so strong there that he can present himself frankly, he (or she) can begin to dance expressively.—I say stomach because the stomach usually faces the audience; one might say waist, groin, or pelvic region.

In looking at Nijinsky pictures, one is struck by the upright tautness about the hips. His waist is broad and powerful. You can see it clearly in the Harlequin pictures. If he is posing on one leg, there is no sense of shifted weight, and as little if he seems to be bending to the side or forward. The effort this means may be compared to lifting a table by one leg and keeping the top horizontal. The center of gravity in the table, and similarly that of his body, has not been shifted. The delicacy with which he cantilevers the weight actually displaced keeps the firmness from being rigidity. I think it is in looking at his waist that one can see best the technical aspect of his instinct for concentrating the origin of movement so that all of it relates to a clear center which is not altered. He keeps the multiplicity, the diffusion which movement has, intelligible by not allowing any doubt as to where the center is. When he moves he does not blur the center of weight in his body; one feels it as clearly as if he were still standing at rest, one can follow its course clearly as it floats about the stage through the dance. And so the motion he makes looks controlled and voluntary and reliable. I imagine it is this constant sense of balance that gave his dancing the unbroken continuity and flow through all the steps and leaps and rests from beginning to end, that critics marveled at.

Incidentally, their remarks of this kind also point to an extraordinary accuracy in his musical timing. For to make the continuity rhythmic as he did, he must have had an unerring instinct at which moment to attack a movement, so that the entire sequence of it would flow as continuously and transform itself into the next motion as securely as did the accompanying sound. To speak of him as unmusical, with no sense of rhythm, as Stravinsky has, is therefore an impropriety that is due to a confusion of meaning in the word "rhythm." The choreography of *Faune* proves that Nijinsky's natural musical intelligence was of the highest order. For this was the first ballet choreography set clearly, not to the measures and periods, but to the expressive flow of the music, to its musical sense. You need only compare *Faune*'s assurance in this respect to the awkwardness musically of Fokine's second scene in *Petrouchka*, the score of which invites the same sort of understanding. But this is not in the photographs.

Nijinsky does not dance from his feet; he dances from his pelvis. The legs do not show off. They have no ornamental pose. Even in his own choreography, though the leg gestures are "composed," they are not treated as pictorial possibilities. They retain their weight. They tell where the body goes and how. But they don't lead it. They are, however, completely expressive in this role; and the thighs in the *Spectre* picture with Karsavina are as full of tenderness as another dancer's face. It is noticeable, too, that Nijinsky's legs are not especially turned out, and a similar moderate *en dehors* seems to be the rule in the Petersburg male dancers of Nijinsky's generation. But the parallel feet in *Narcisse* and *Faune*, and the pigeon toes in *Til* are not a willful contradiction of the academic principle for the sake of something new. They can, it seems to me, be properly understood only by a turned-out dancer, as Nijinsky himself clearly was. For the strain of keeping the pelvis in the position the ballet dancer holds it in for balance is much greater with parallel or turned-in feet (which contradict the outward twist of the thigh); and this strain gives a new plastic dimension to the legs and feet, if it is carried through as forcefully as Nijinsky does.—I am interested, too, to notice that in standing Nijinsky does not press his weight mostly on the ball of the big toe, but grips the floor with the entire surface of the foot.

I have neglected to mention the hands, which are alive and simple, with more expression placed in the wrist than the fingers. They are not at all "Italian"; and are full of variety without an emphasis on sensitivity. The hands in *Spectre* are celebrated, and remind one of the hands in Picassos ten years later. I am also very moved by the uplifted, half-unclenched hands in the *Jeux* picture, as mysterious as breathing in sleep. One can see, too, that in *Petrouchka* the hands are black-mittened, not white-mittened as now; the new costume makes the dance against the black wall in the second scene a foolish hand dance, instead of a dance of a whole figure, as intended.

The manner in which Nijinsky's face changes from role to role is immediately striking. It is enhanced by make-up, but not created by it. In fact, a friend pointed out that the only role in which one recognizes Nijinsky's civilian face is that of Petrouchka where he is most heavily made up. There is no mystery about such transformability. People don't usually realize how much any face changes in the course of a day, and how often it is unrecognizable for an instant or two. Nijinsky seems to have controlled the variability a face has. The same metamorphosis is obvious in his body. The Spectre, for instance, has no age or sex, the Faun is adolescent, the hero of *Jeux* has a body full-grown and experienced. Til can be either boy or man. The Slave in *Scheherazade* is fat, the Spectre is thin. It does not look like the same body. One can say that in this sense there is no exhibitionism in Nijinsky's photographs. He is never showing you himself, or an interpretation of himself. He is never vain of what he is showing you. The audience does not see him as a professional dancer, or as a professional charmer. He disappears completely, and instead there is an imaginary being in his place. Like a classic artist, he remains detached, unseen, unmoved, disinterested. Looking at him, one is in an imaginary world, entire and very clear; and one's emotions are not directed at their material objects, but at their imaginary satisfactions. As he said himself, he danced with love.

To sum up, Nijinsky in his photographs shows us the style of a classic artist. The emotion he projects, the character he projects is not communicated as his own, but as one that exists independently of himself, in the objective world. Similarly his plastic sense suggests neither a private yearning into an infinity of space nor a private shutting out of surrounding relationships; both of them legitimate romantic attitudes. The weight he gives his own body, the center which he gives his plastic motions, strikes a balance with the urge and rapidity of leaps and displacements. It strikes a balance between the role he dances and the roles of his partners. The distinction of place makes the space look real, the distinction of persons makes the drama real. And for the sake of this clarification he characterizes (or mimes, one might say) even such a conventional ornamental show-off, or "pure dance," part as that in *Pavillon*. On the other hand, the awkward heaviness that *Faune, Sacre*, and *Jeux* exhibited, and that was emphasized by their angular precision, was not, I believe, an anticlassic innovation. It was an effort to make the dance more positive, to make clearer still the center of gravity of a movement, so that its extent, its force, its direction, its elevation can be appreciated not incidentally merely, but integrally as drama. He not only extended the plastic range in dancing, but clarified it. And this is the way to give meaning to dancing; not secondhand literary meaning, but direct meaning. Nijinsky's latest intentions of "circular movement," and the improvisational quality Til seems to have had are probably a normal development of his sense of motion in relation to a point of repose—a motion that grew more animated and diverse as his instinct became more exercised. (An evolution not wholly dissimilar can be followed in Miss Graham's work, for instance.) And I consider the following remark he made to be indicative of the direction of his instinct: "La grace, le charme, le joli sont rangés tout autour du point central qu'est le beau. C'est pour le beau que je travaille." I do not see anything in these pictures that would lead one to suppose that Nijinsky's subsequent insanity cast any premonitory shadow on his phenomenally luminous dance intelligence.

These notes are not meant to be exhaustive, but to invite you to look at the pictures attentively. There is much to enjoy in them. I mentioned another aspect of them in *Modern*

Music: "He looks as if the body remembered the whole dance, all the phases of it, as he holds the one pose; he seems to be thinking, I've just done that, and then after this I do that, and then that, and then comes that; so his body looks like a face lighting up at a single name that evokes a whole crowd of remembered friends." This small album of his photographs is intended to take the place for the present of a book that I hope Mr. Paul Magriel will be able to assemble after the war, from all over the world: a book presenting a complete photographic record. We have included here a snapshot of Nijinsky leaping high. Few of the other pictures seem to be action shots. Several of those by de Meyer are not even poses literally from the dances, but seem invented to give a sense of the general tone of the role. I do not think this vitiates their accuracy in showing Nijinsky's style of dancing, or of characterization. The sureness of invention they show helps us to see why as a dancer he was, to the most intelligent public of his time, unparalleled.

In their stillness Nijinsky's pictures have more vitality than the dances they remind us of as we now see them on the stage. They remain to show us what dancing can be; and what the spectator and the dancer each aspire to, and hold to be a fair standard of art. I think they give the discouraged dance lover faith in dancing as a serious human activity. As Mr. Van Vechten wrote after seeing him in 1916: "His dancing has the unbroken quality of music, the balance of great painting, the meaning of fine literature, and the emotion inherent in all these arts."

Left: Nijinsky, ca. 1900.
Right: Nijinsky, ca. 1908. (In cadet
uniform of the Imperial Russian Ballet
School).

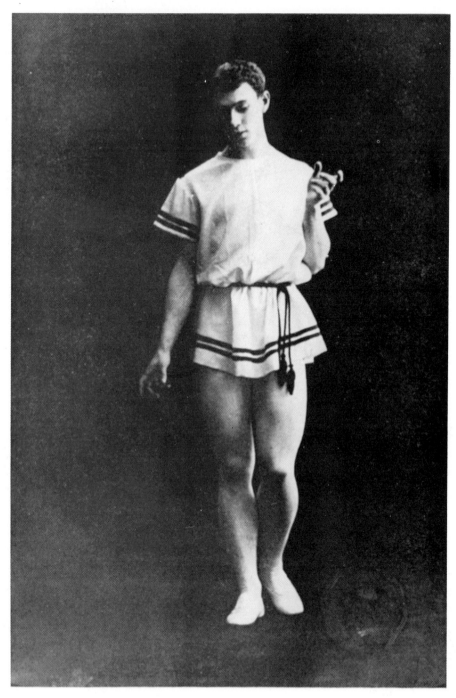

Nijinsky in *Eunice*. St. Petersburg, 1907.

Nijinsky. K. A. Fischer, St. Petersburg, 1907.

Nijinsky in *Le Pavillon d'Armide*. St. Petersburg, 1907.

Nijinsky in *Giselle*. Paris, 1911.   Nijinsky with Karsavina in *Giselle*. Paris, 1911.

Nijinsky in *King Candaule*. St. Petersburg, 1908.   Nijinsky in *Giselle*. St. Petersburg, 1909.

Upper: Nijinsky in *Le Pavillon d'Armide.* Paris, 1909. Lower: Nijinsky in *Le Pavillon d'Armide with* Pavlova. St. Petersburg, 1907.

Nijinsky in *Le Pavillon d'Armide*. De Meyer, Paris, 1911. Upper right: Action snapshot.

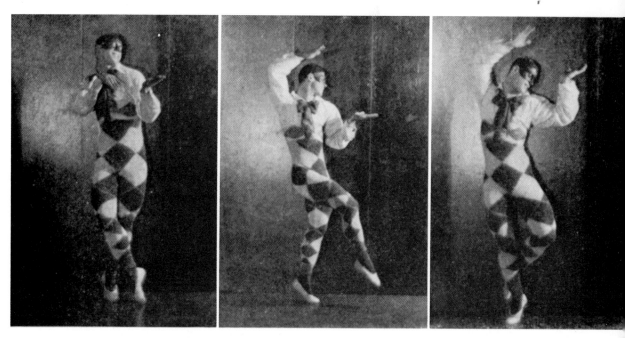

Nijinsky in *Carnaval*. De Meyer, Paris, 1910.

Nijinsky in *Scheherazade*. De Meyer, Paris, 1910.

Nijinsky in *Le Festin*. Bert, Paris, 1911.

Nijinsky in *Les Orientales*. Druet, Paris, 1911.

Nijinsky in *Le Spectre de la Rose*. Hoppe, Paris, 1911.

Nijinsky in *Spectre de la Rose*. Lower:
With Karsavina, Paris, 1911.

Nijinsky in *Le Dieu Bleu. Comoedia Illustré*, Paris, 1912.

Nijinsky in *L'Après-midi D'un Faune*. De Meyer, Paris, 1911.

Nijinsky in *Petrouchka*. Elliott & Fry, London, 1911.

Nijinsky in *Les Orientales*. Paris, 1911.

Nijinsky in *Jeux.* Gerschel, Paris, 1913.

Nijinsky in *Jeux*. Upper left and lower, with Karsavina and Shollar. Paris, 1911.

Nijinsky in *Narcisse*. Paris, 1911.

Upper left and lower:
Nijinsky with Karsavina
in *Zobeide*. Berlin, 1914.
Upper right: With Kar-
savina in *Scheherazade*.
Berlin, 1914.

Nijinsky in practice clothes. St. Petersburg, 1908.

Nijinsky. White, New York, 1916.

Nijinsky as *Til Eulenspiegel*. New York, 1916.

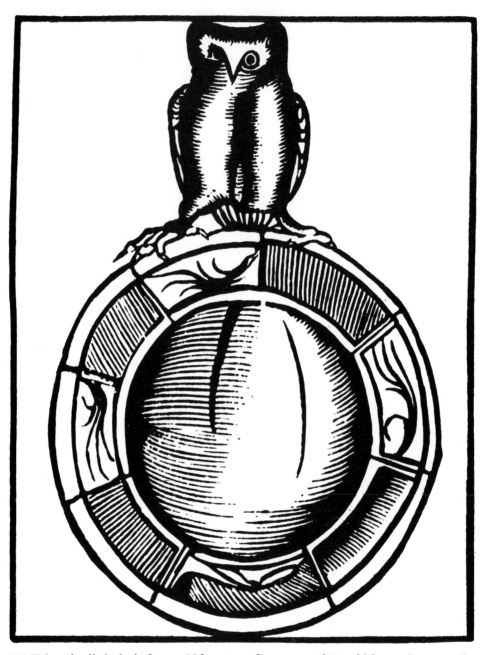

Til Eulenspiegel's insignia from a 15th century German woodcut, which was drawn on the curtain for the ballet.

NIJINSKY AND
TIL EULENSPIEGEL

BY ROBERT EDMOND JONES

The question is not yet settled, whether much that is glorious—whether all that is profound—does not spring . . . from moods of mind exalted at the expense of the general intellect.
—Poe's *Eleonora*

IN 1916 a diffident young man from New Hampshire who was just beginning to make his way in New York as a stage designer was commissioned by Vaslav Nijinsky to design the décor for a new ballet. Up to that time no American designer had been so honored. I was that young man, and I am going to set down as carefully as possible my recollections of this great dancer and choreographer—now, alas! a living legend—and of an experience so novel and so startling that it altered the course of my entire life.

Not all of my story is pleasant. It is a story of two differing temperaments—of two differing cultures, really—unexpectedly and violently thrown into contact with one another. In the ballet *Til Eulenspiegel*, the artistic approach of old Russia and the artistic approach of new America met and fused for the first time in theater history. The result—it must be stated at the outset—was an instant and emphatic success. Since that day many dramatic events have been taking place in the world. Now, in this year of grace 1945, it would appear that that old Russia and new America are destined to march side by side toward a radiant future. But at the time of this association such a rapport was undreamed of, and it fell to me to bear the full brunt of the initial impact of the Russian temperament, to take it, so to speak, head on. Certain details of this experience seem to me in retrospect not unlike the custard-pie scenes in an old Mack Sennett comedy.

I shall set down my story in a series of pictures, like the "flashbacks" of a cinema, as they appeared to me at the time, without benefit of a maturer judgment. Some of the story is sordid, some of it is humiliating, some of it is outrageous. But all of it is marvelous, and all of it is alive.

The first picture: It is the afternoon of a late spring day in 1916, hot and humid. I sit in the drawing room of Emilie Hapgood, the president of the now-defunct New York Stage Society. Curtains are drawn against the breathless heat. The room—all ivory-white and pale silks—is in semidarkness. We converse in low voices, waiting. Presently Nijinsky and Mme. Nijinsky are announced. I see, first, an extremely pretty young woman, fashionably dressed in black, and, following her, a small, somewhat stocky young man walking with delicate birdlike steps—precise, a dancer's walk. He is very nervous. His eyes are troubled. He looks eager, anxious, excessively intelligent. He seems tired, bored, excited, all at once. I observe that he has a disturbing habit of picking at the flesh on the side of his thumbs until they bleed. Through all my memories of this great artist runs the recurring image of those raw red thumbs. He broods and dreams, goes far away into reverie, returns again. At intervals his face lights up with a brief, dazzling smile. His manner is simple, ingratiating, so direct as to be almost humble. I like him at once. Tales of unusual accomplishments and unusual ardors have clustered around this man as honeybees cluster about a perfumed flower. There was something about a scarf. There was something about a banquet. There was something about a leap through a window. There was something. . . . But that was then and this is now. I see no trace in him of the legendary exotic. Here is only the straightforward and matter-of-fact approach of the newly appointed maestro of the Russian Ballet who has an idea and wants to see it carried out.

I realize at once that I am in the presence of a genius. What, precisely, does one mean by this word, so often and so carelessly used? Miss Gertrude Stein, who by her own account of herself would seem to know, defines it (I quote from memory) as the ability to talk and listen at the same time. This particular attribute of Nijinsky's genius is not evident at the moment, since he and I are struggling to communicate our ideas to one another in extremely halting French. I sense, however, a quality in him which I can define here only as a continual preoccupation with standards of excellence so high that they are really not of this world. This artist, it is clear, concerns himself with incredible perfections. I sense, too, the extraordinary nervous energy of the man—an almost frightening awareness, a curious mingling of eagerness and apprehension. The atmosphere he brings with him is—how shall I say?— *oppressive.* There is in him an astonishing drive, a mental engine, too high-powered, racing —perhaps even now—to its final breakdown. Otherwise there is nothing of the abnormal about him. Only an impression of something too eager, too brilliant, a quivering of the nerves, a nature racked to dislocation by a merciless creative urge. And those raw thumbs.

I show the maestro a portfolio of my designs for various stage productions. There are costume sketches for *The Man Who Married a Dumb Wife*, the stage settings for *The Devil's Garden* and *The Happy Ending*, recently produced by Arthur Hopkins, some notes for *Les Précieuses Ridicules*, the project for Shelley's *Cenci* worked out during my *Wanderjahr* in Germany. It is obvious that Nijinsky thinks that I am a beginner—indeed, I am one—but I can see that he is interested in my drawings. There is something in them that he may be able to use. We sit side by side on the carpet in the center of the shadowy room, turning over the leaves of the portfolio. "Très heureux," he says, politely. . . . The couple departs. I am left in an agony of anticipation. Dare I hope? . . . Could it be? . . . I wonder . . . if only—!

Another picture: I am accepted—I am a happy boy this day—and I am sent to Bar Harbor to collaborate with the maestro on the creation of the new ballet. I am quartered in a huge old-fashioned summer hotel, all piazzas and towers, with curving driveways and mammoth beds of angry red cannas on the lawns. Nijinsky lives there, too, with his pretty wife—always a little *souffrante* from the heat—and an enchanting girl baby with oblique Mongolian eyes like her father's. He practices hard and long during the day with his accompanist in the lovely little Greek temple set among the pines by the shore of the bay. In the evenings we work together until far into the night. And how we work!

Coming on the heels of the most striking series of novelties in America for the last ten years, Til Eulenspiegel *stood in a class by itself as a combination of musical, pictorial, and terpsichorean art.* . . . How shall I tell of this long-forgotten ballet, so fresh, so natural, so innocent, that flashed and vanished like a fevered dream? No critic, with the exception of H. T. Parker of the Boston *Transcript*, seems to have been able to appreciate it at the time in its true relation to the other works in the Diaghilev repertoire. It was too original in its conception, too novel, too seldom performed. Relatively few people saw it, it was soon gone, and now it is only a memory. But without question it showed Nijinsky at the very height of his creative power, and I believe it to have been one of the few genuine masterpieces—I use the word deliberately—in the entire recorded history of ballet.

Perhaps the clearest and simplest way to give the reader an impression of the finished work is to quote from Robert Bagar's excellent synopsis, *The Story of the Ballet Music:*

A strong sense of German folk-feeling pervades the whole work; the source from which the tone-poet drew his inspiration is clearly indicated in the introductory bars. . . . To some extent this stands for the "once upon a time" of the story books. That what follows is not to be treated in the pleasant and agreeable manner of narrative poetry, but in a more sturdy fashion, is at once made apparent by a characteristic bassoon figure which breaks in *sforzato* upon the *piano* of the strings. Of equal import-ance for the development of the piece is the immediately following humorous horn theme. . . . Begin-ning quietly and gradually becoming more lively, it is at first heard against a tremolo of the "divided" violins and then again in the *tempo primo*. . . .

Here he (Til) is (clarinet phrase followed by chord for wind instruments). He wanders through the land as a thoroughgoing adventurer. His clothes are tattered and torn: a queer, fragmentary version of the Eulenspiegel motive resounds from the horns. Following a merry play with this im-portant leading motive, which directly leads to a short but brilliant *tutti*, in which it again asserts itself, first in the flutes, and then finally merges into a softly-murmuring and extended tremolo for the violas, this same motive, gracefully phrased, reappears in succession in the basses, flute, first violins, and again in the basses. The rogue, putting on his best manners, slyly passes through the gate, and enters a certain city. It is market-day; the women sit at their stalls and the plattle (flutes, oboes, and clarinets). Hop! Eulenspiegel springs on his horse (indicated by rapid triplets extending through three measures, from the low D of the bass clarinet to the highest A of the D clarinet), gives a smack of his whip, and rides into the midst of the crowd. Clink, clash, clatter! A confused sound of broken pots and pans, and the market-women are put to flight. In haste the rascal rides away (as is admirably illustrated by a *fortissimo* passage for the trombones) and secures a safe retreat.

This was his first merry prank; a second follows immediately. . . . Eulenspiegel has put on the vestments of a priest, and assumes a very unctuous mien. Though posing as a preacher of morals, the rogue peeps out from the folds of his mantle (the Eulenspiegel motive on the clarinet points to the imposture). He fears for the success of his scheme. A figure played by muted violins, horns and trum-pets makes it plain that he does not feel comfortable in his borrowed plumes.

But soon he makes up his mind. Away with all scruples! He tears them off (solo, violin, *glissando*).

Again the Eulenspiegel theme is brought forward in the previous lively tempo, but is now subtly metamorphosed and chivalrously colored. Eulenspiegel has become a Don Juan, and he waylays pretty women. And one has bewitched him: Eulenspiegel is in love. Hear how now, glowing with love, the violins, clarinets, and flutes sing. But in vain. His advances are received with derision, and he goes away in a rage. How can one treat him so slightingly? Is he not a splendid fellow? Vengeance on the whole human race!

He gives vent to his rage in a *fortissimo* of horns in unison followed by a pause, and strange per-sonages suddenly draw near ('cellos). A troop of honest, worthy Philistines!

In an instant all his anger is forgotten. But it is still his chief joy to make fun of these lords and protectors of blameless decorum, to mock them, as is apparent from the lively and accentuated fragments of the theme, sounded at the beginning by the horn, which are now heard first from horns, violins, 'cellos, and then from trumpets, oboes, and flutes. Now that Eulenspiegel has had his joke, he goes away and leaves the professors and doctors behind in thoughtful meditation. Fragments of the typical theme of the Philistines are here treated canonically. . . .

If we take a formal view, we have now reached the repetition of the chief theme. A merry jester, a born liar, Eulenspiegel goes wherever he can succeed with a hoax. His insolence knows no bounds. Alas! there is a sudden jolt to his wanton humor. The drum rolls a hollow roll; the jailer drags the rascally prisoner into the criminal court. The verdict "guilty" is thundered against the brazen-faced knave.

The Eulenspiegel theme replies calmly to the threatening chords of wind and lower strings. Eulenspiegel lies. Again the threatening tones resound; but Eulenspiegel does not confess his guilt. On the contrary, he lies for the third time. His jig is up. Fear seizes him. The Hypocrisy motive is sounded piteously; the fatal moment draws near; his hour has struck! The descending leap of a minor seventh in bassoons, horns, trombones, tuba, betokens his death. He is danced in air. A last struggle (flutes), and his soul takes flight.

After a sad, tremulous *pizzicato* of the strings the epilogue begins. At first it is almost identical with the introductory measures, which are repeated in full; then the most essential parts of the second and third chief-theme passages appear, and finally merge into the soft chord of the sixth on A-flat, while woodwinds and violins sustain. Eulenspiegel has become a legendary character. The people tell their tales about him; 'Once upon a time. . . .' But that he was a merry rogue and a real devil of a fellow seems to be expressed by the final eight measures, full orchestra, *fortissimo*.

The character of the spectacle itself is suggested by this excerpt from *Legends of the Ballets*, by Frederick A. King:

With Puck as his nearest analogue in English literature, Mr. Nijinsky brings forward out of German folk-lore the figure of the rogue whose pranks set at naught the customs and conventions of the common-place people. He flits in and out of the market place of a mediaeval town, appearing successively as a buffoon, a clergyman, a knight and a professor, in each instance mocking the populace and mystifying their regulated minds in whom the routine of life admits of no deviations. His inflammatory speeches stir the people to anger and he is arrested and brought before a judge. Here again he only mocks and his reward is a sentence to die upon the gallows. After his death the people are overcome with remorse; they remember his bright sallies, his gleaming wit, his fascinating presence, and their minds are not composed until his spirit appears and assures them he will live forever in the hearts of the people.

The ballet was devised and elaborated by Mr. Nijinsky during his recent confinement in Austria as a prisoner of war. Mr. Strauss, whose scores have already been utilized by the Russians in their

Nijinsky in *Til Eulenspiegel*. New York, 1916.

ballets, readily lent his assent to the use of this one, and even volunteered to alter the reading of the score to adapt it to the exigencies of choreographic treatment. To this proposal, however, Mr. Nijinsky replied that no necessity would require such a step, as he had already visualized the entire action from the original.

Nijinsky's energy, his ardor, his daring, his blazing imagination, by turns fantastic, gorgeous, grotesque, are a source of continual astonishment and delight to me. His conception of this ballet is vastly new and different. A consummate actor, he changes, chameleon-like, from moment to moment as he talks. Now he is a child, wide-eyed and mischievous, now a jeering zany, now a lover, tender and pleading, now a demoniac figure from a medieval Dance of Death. Always he is repeating the phrase, "Pour faire rire, pour faire rire." He summons the spirits of Breughel, of Munchhausen, of Rabelais. Gargantua and Pantagruel peer over his shoulder. Everything in this ballet is to be gay, athletic, coarse, animal. An irresistible comicality breathes through it all, a light deft fresh movement, a ripple of mocking laughter. At times it seems not so much a ballet as an embodied romp. "Pour faire rire, pour faire rire. . . ."

The maestro is at my elbow. I draw. He watches, criticizes, exhorts. Together we map out the design for the front curtain—a huge sheet of parchment emblazoned with Til's device of the owl and the looking glass, all blurred and worn, like a page torn from a long-forgotten manuscript of the Middle Ages. The market place of Braunschweig begins to take shape in front of the brooding black mass of the cathedral, a Braunschweig seen through Til's own eyes. We fill the square with flaunting gay color. I sketch the rosy-cheeked apple-woman with her big basket of apples, all red and green and russet; the cloth merchant in his shop; the fat blond baker with his long loaves of bread; the scrawny sweetmeat seller, decked out in peppermint stripes of red and white, like one of his own candies; the cobbler carrying his rack of oddly shaped shoes; the burghers, the priests, the professors in their long robes and their ridiculous shovel hats; the street urchins and the beggars; the three chatelaines, taking the air beneath peaked hennins that tower a full six feet above their heads, their trains streaming away ten feet, twenty feet, thirty feet behind them . . . and Til himself in his varied disguises—Til the imp, Til the lover, Til the scholar, Til flouting, taunting, imploring, writhing in his death agonies. . . .

The hours fly past. Wild, eager, anxious hours.

Invitations to lunch and dine at the great houses of Bar Harbor are showered upon me like a rain of gold. At first I am overwhelmed by this unexpected and profuse hospitality, but I soon realize that I am being sought after only in order that my various hosts and hostesses may induce me to bring the great dancer to their tables. Some of these invitations are on a lower social plane. One morning the maestro and I are invited to the fashionable swimming pool. After our swim we dress in adjoining little wooden cabanas. I am partly dressed. I hear a light tap at the door. I open it. A middle-aged man stands there, exquisitely dressed in fastidious nuances of pearl gray which harmonize with the tones of his silvery, scented mustache. He is tall and willowy and his delicate hands are beautifully manicured. We look at one another. No word is spoken. Presently he takes a large flat case of pearl-gray leather from his pocket, opens the lid and holds the case out to me. On a bed of pearl-gray velvet lies a mass of beautiful jewels—moonstones, black pearls, diamonds, emeralds, cabochon rubies. . . . There is an awkward silence. Time seems to run down and stand still, like a worn-out alarm clock, like a tired heart that stops beating. I hear Nijinsky putting on his shoes in the next compartment. The stranger in gray holds out his store of fabulous baubles, all glittering and flashing in the acrid New England sunlight. All at once I burst out laughing. He closes the door, turns on his heel, and silently goes away.

Another picture: We are in New York once more and rehearsals are beginning in earnest. I spend many hours with Nijinsky and his company on the bare stage of the old Manhattan Opera House. The wonderful music of Moussorgsky and Rimsky-Korsakov pervades the air. It is new to me. I breathe it in, and I tremble. I am ill with excitement. Mystical winds blow over river valleys. Conflagrations of color blaze on faraway mountains. Spilt blood dries on daggers of cold steel. Violins torture and sting. I hear cries and sobs. Always death is in the air—cruel death, bitter death. Always the eternal farewells. . . . I go through the days in a dream. Can life indeed be so rich, so splendid, so passionate? Even now, after twenty-nine years, the reveries of those enchanted hours come back to me and I am lost once more in the horizons of the mysterious lands that Glinka and Borodin knew.

The scale model for the setting is finished. The designs for the costumes are likewise finished and approved. Now comes the first difficulty, the first sign of friction. A storm is gathering. Why is it, someone has asked, that birth is always painful and rarely lovely?

In this country when scenery is to be painted, the various "drops" and "flats" of canvas are stretched on frames, like huge easels, which hang at the sides of the scenic studios and are raised or lowered through slots cut in the floor by means of ropes and pulleys and counter-

A. Costume sketch for *Chatelaine*.

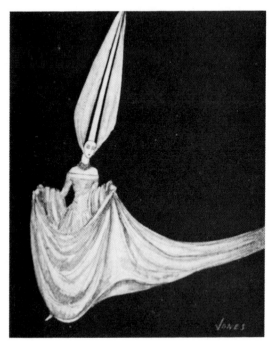

B. Costume sketch for *Til*.

Costume sketch for *The Professors.*

weights. In Russia, however, the method of scene painting is quite different. The drops and flats are simply laid flat on the floor and the painters, wearing carpet slippers, roam about over them carrying great pails of color and long-handled brushes, like brooms. Nijinsky, quite naturally, wishes the setting for *Til* to be executed in the Russian manner, *sur planché*. But alas! there is no one in New York who knows how to paint in this style. Work is accordingly started in the conventional American manner in the West Side studios of Dodge & Castle. When Nijinsky hears of this he orders the work stopped at once.

The next picture shows the maestro riding toward the scenic studio in a taxi with me through a Negro district known as San Juan Hill, after the bloody battleground of that name in the Spanish War. A director of the Metropolitan Opera sits between us. We are silent and tense. The studio is at the foot of a hill by the Hudson. As we descend the hill a Negress is carried shrieking out of a doorway, spouting blood from a dozen razor slashes on her head and arms. A bad omen? I wonder. . . .

We go up steep narrow winding stairs to the scene loft. This is a long, narrow and extremely high space with walls of dirty whitewashed brick. The paint frames hang from cables along the wall at either side. Tall, narrow windows are set high up at either end. The air is charged with a strong, almost nauseating smell of fish glue. Underneath the windows stand rough wooden cabinets, like bookshelves, on which are arranged dozens upon dozens of white china *pots de chambre* filled to overflowing with colored pigments in bewildering variety—gamboge, raw umber, ultramarine, orange mineral, rose madder, vert émeraude. . . . Half a dozen painters—"artists" is their traditional title—we still say, "Job for the artist!" or "Hey, artist!"—looking in their dirty white overalls not unlike a band of White Wings, hold others of these useful receptacles, into which they dip their paintbrushes from time to time, applying streaks of paint in vivid colors to the great sheets of canvas stretched on the frames at either side of the loft. It is all rather like a Freudian dream in which one sees with horror one's deepest and most forbidden repressions dragged howling into the harsh light of day. Nijinsky gives a wild look about him. His eyes swivel in his head. Is *this* the way stage settings are painted in "les pays des barbares"? He mutters something unintelligible. The incongruity of the occasion strikes all three of us at the same instant. We shout with hysterical laughter. The tension is broken. "C'est vraiment très heureux," the maestro says with a giggle. We ride up the hill again, relaxed and friendly now. We return to the rehearsal. I am only too content to let the matter rest. But through my mind runs a phantasmagoria of conflicting images—the figure of the dreaming faun, a rose petal

Sketch for the set of *Til Eulenspiegel*. Collection of Fred Schang.

drifting through a moonlit window in a soft summer night, star-drenched banquets at the Lido, répétitions générales in Paris with languid balletomanes from the Côte d'Azur sighing and shuddering, raw red thumbs, winding stairs, *pots de chambre* splashed with hues of more-than-Oriental splendor, White Wings, rivers of blood on a sidewalk. . . . How will it end?

Another picture rises in the memory. Etched in acid, this one. I am unexpectedly summoned to the Opera House. The completed setting for *Til Eulenspiegel* is standing on the stage. I glance at it quickly as I pass. Not bad, I say to myself. I sense an obscurely hostile atmosphere in the theater. I am escorted to Nijinsky's dressing room.

The walls (I remember to this day) are papered in stripes of two tones of violent red. There is a pier glass and a chaise longue. On the dressing table a number of stilettolike knives, sharpened to a razor edge, are ranged in an orderly row. The maestro is waiting for me in a flame of rage. Torrents of Russian imprecations pour from his lips. The open door fills with frowning alien faces. Nijinsky switches to broken French. He lashes out at me with an insensate blind hate. It is a nightmare set in a blast furnace. I gather that in his opinion America is, of all countries in the world, the most backward in every aspect of its culture, that the level of artistic achievement on this side of the Atlantic Ocean is not only beneath notice but beneath contempt, and that Destiny has selected me—me!—from out of America's countless millions to symbolize, eternally and ineffaceably, everything that is most benighted in our so-called civilization. Since that day I have had occasion to hear these same views aired more than once. I still cannot believe that they are true.

Presently Nijinsky pauses out of sheer exhaustion. We go back to the stage. The setting stands there, dejected, like a child that has been punished. Swift curt commands are issued. Stagehands hale the accursed thing from sight, swing it into the flies, flatten it against the back wall of the theater. A shattered dream, a house of cards demolished. . . . The rehearsal begins, belated and listless. The rhythms falter, the air seems duller than Saturnian lead. Suddenly there is a cry. The maestro stumbles and falls. He has sprained his ankle. He is carried moaning and cursing to his suite at the Biltmore Hotel. "Your scenery is so bad," a dancer says to me, "that when our maestro saw it he fell down." Eager throats take up the refrain: "Yes, your scenery is so bad that when our maestro saw it he fell down."

I am a very discouraged boy indeed.

At the theater the next morning my limitations as an artist are enlarged upon by the

Nijinsky applying make-up to one of the corps de ballet. New York, 1916.

manager of the company with an unusual clarity and a notable absence of sentiment. The principal defects of the setting, I am made to understand, are, first, that it is too shallow—it does not allow enough space for the evolutions of the dancers—and, second, that it is not high enough to give the effect of crazy exaggeration the maestro had visualized. The first defect is remedied by the simple expedient of placing the setting farther back on the stage. The second problem is not so easily solved. After a consultation (I can never forget this half hour!) it is agreed that a piece of canvas ten feet high is to be added at the base of each of the two flats which represent the houses of the town, and that this space is to be painted with an impression of foliage in broad washes of ultramarine. The flats are strung up on the frames at the rear of the stage, and with the aid of a paint boy I elongate the trees of Braunschweig, trying in vain to ignore the audible disapproval of the ensemble rehearsing below.

The next picture: Two days have elapsed. The première has been postponed. Again I am summoned to the maestro's presence. It is evening. Nijinsky lies in bed, *maladif*, drenched in pathos, sad as a dying prince out of a drama by Maeterlinck. The little room is crowded to suffocation with the entire ensemble of the ballet, fully dressed in the costumes of *Til Eulenspiegel*. They stare at me silently with black hatred in their faces. Now begins a scene compared to which the earlier scene in the dressing room at the Opera House seems but the remote faded echo of an old refrain. This one is good. The maestro really puts his heart into it this time. The occasion—as Robert Benchley has since said of another and quite different occasion—has all the easy informality of a prairie fire. Shoes are wrenched from the feet of the *coryphées*, necklaces are torn from their throats and shattered into fragments against the walls. Unbelievable insults are hurled at me. It is like taking the lid off hell.

This, I say to myself, is what it means to have one's back to the wall, facing a firing squad. *Have you no mercy? No mercy. . . .* This is what it means to be whipped at the triangles. *A low murmur ran through the ranks as the scarcely healed backs were laid bare for the second time to receive the lash. . . .* This is what it means to stand in the deathcart, jolting over cobblestones, on the way to the guillotine. *Along the streets the death carts rumble, hollow and harsh. . . . The murmuring of many voices, the upturning of many faces, the pressing of many footsteps in the outskirts of the crowd, so that it swells forward in a mass. . . .*

Here I am, alone and unknown, in a little room at the Biltmore Hotel, in the midst of a lurid fantasy of the Middle Ages—a fantasy of my own making—with one of the world's greatest artists shrieking at me. There is no escape. There is no hope. This is the end. Nothing. Nowhere. Never.

Then something happens inside me. Something old and cold and ancestral rises up in me. The sense of the occasion strikes me with a kind of wry humor. As I look about me at the gaily costumed crowd I know with a definite inner conviction that this ballet will be a success. There is something about the American public, there is a quality of appreciation, a peculiarly American point of view, that even these artists, remarkable though they are, cannot yet understand. I think at this bitter moment my belief in myself as an artist is born. I will see this thing through. And then—

Another picture: A week later. The dress rehearsal of *Til Eulenspiegel* is scheduled for two o'clock in the afternoon. I enter the auditorium of the Opera House by the front door. The curtain is up. On the stage stands my setting—my setting, mine!—remote, complete, fully lighted, all glowing with jewellike blues and greens. All up and down on either side of the proscenium the great gilded boxes are filled with the dancers, dressed and painted, waiting for the ballet to begin. The circular lunette in the ceiling of the auditorium has been temporarily removed for repairs and a shaft of sunlight, pure gold, streams down across the boxes, turning the proscenium into a spectacle out of dreamland. It is exceedingly beautiful.

The boxes glitter and flame and the palaces of Braunschweig tower up out of burning blue dusk into a haze of violet and rose. A fountain of music wells up from the orchestra, a shower of sparkling notes. . . .

The torment is over. My life in the theater has begun in earnest. *Ah, light, and flame, and flowers! Ah, starry meadows beyond Orion! Ah, fields of the triplicate suns!*

The relief from the strain of the last weeks is too great. My head seems to burst. Spots and bars of gold dance before my eyes.

I faint dead away.

Now the final picture, the first performance seen from the wings. There is a bustle, a tremor, a sickening moment of suspense. The orchestra strikes up the first bars of the music. The great curtain slides upward sighing into the shadows far overhead, where half-seen electricians move along the light-bridges hung with many-colored lamps, like constellations of stars. *An astonishing congeries of forms and colors assails the eye, grotesque, impossible figments of an imagination enchained by some ludicrous nightmare, as it were, but engrossing and appropriate beyond belief. A species of whimsicality run riot sets before the astonished vision a medieval town that never was in any age and laves it with nocturnal blue touched with shafts of crepuscular light which illuminates the inverted cornucopia roofs of tiny houses tilted at crazy angles and suggesting for all the world sheaves of skyrockets. A wondertown in a wonderland. . . . The personages might have stepped out of some Volksbuch of the Middle Ages. But there is no suggestion of coloristic disharmony within the somber scenic frame: and the light on the figurants is magical. . . .* I hear a crash of applause, fierce and frightening. The little figure in green begins its leapings and laughings. There is the scene of wild love-making, the confutation of the scholars, the strange solo dance, swift as the flash of a rapier, the hanging of the corpse on the gibbet—and last of all, the apparition of the ghost shooting upward through a foam of tiny lanterns, like a moth veering above a sea of fireflies. . . . Then the triumph, and the cheering, like the clamor of great bells—now rapturous, now softening, melting—and the mountains of flowers, and the curtain calls that seem never to end. Nijinsky and I bow together, hand in hand. He is all smiles. As the curtain sweeps upward for the last time he murmurs once more, "C'est vraiment très, très heureux."

I go home. I am finished with it all.

I never see him again.

Now my story is ended and these memories fade into the past. The great artist who taught me so much now exists apart, away from us, in a sad world of his own. I dwell for the last time upon my strange, magical, shattering experience and remember once more what it has meant to me in the years that have passed since the creation of *Til Eulenspiegel*. It has given me a heightened and broadened sense of life. It has taught me to be true to my own inner dream, to live by this dream, and never to betray it.

And it has taught me, I hope, to be kind.

Til Eulenspiegel. 15th Century German Woodcut.
Collection of Joseph Cornell.

APPENDICES

NOTE ON NIJINSKY
AND ROBERT EDMOND JONES

BY STARK YOUNG

FOR WEEKS once in London I saw every performance that the company of the Russian Ballet gave. They had not been very long out of Russia then and were at their peak. Diaghilev's hand was on everything, and there was a completeness, a unity, a varied singleness of perfection in the case of each production, or shall we say composition, or performance, that I had never seen before and have never seen since. From all that brilliant assemblage the figure, of course, who stood out most was Nijinsky. I have in my time seen a few, a very few, artists of the theater who were more profound, more infinitely human, and more tragic to the heart and mind, but I have never seen any other artist so varied in his compulsion, so absorbing in his variety, so glamorous in his stage presence as was Nijinsky.

From time to time I have been tempted to write of Nijinsky and have been invited to do so, but it has seemed to me that lacking his presence all the words I could conjure up would be more or less futile and would resolve themselves into a mass and aspect of gush not unlike our grandfathers' critics when they spoke of their great sopranos. It is amazing to see how Mr. Jones has avoided that pitfall.

The article by Mr. Jones seems to me notable for several reasons. In the first place, it is an account of Nijinsky under quite a different guise from that in which I saw him, when he was protected by Diaghilev, shielded from every intrusion, directed, instructed, perfected, and guarded as no other artist I ever heard of has been. When Mr. Jones worked with Nijinsky he dealt with a great artist who was acting also as maestro. The whole situation thus becomes enormously different. This difference has a significant bearing not only on the ballet that Mr. Jones records but on the nature of art itself, and the article is therefore doubly important.

There must be few people indeed who know anything about our theater who do not consider Mr. Robert Edmond Jones not only the first and leading figure in the history of its décor, but also its most fecundative and luminous mind and spirit. The article is, therefore, not only an account of the great artist that Nijinsky was but of the first wings and certainty of a fine artist of our own.

THE STRANGENESS OF TIL

BY H. T. PARKER

NECESSARILY a mimed tale, so full and various of action and suggestion as is Mr. Nijinsky's choreographic fable, can leave but confused impression in a single seeing. First of all, it was plain last evening that Strauss's rondo of like title is no more than background to the whole, like Debussy's music in the mimed episode of the faun or Schumann's among the fancies of *Butterflies*. Once and again it rhythmed the dancers and mimes as in the passage that celebrates Til's love-making; here and there the acute intelligence and the ingenious invention of Mr. Nijinsky gave a musical turn to the action as when the learned pedants answer the jeers of Til in a kind of scholarly counterpoint. Momentarily, too, the accent of this action was the accent of the music; but usually Strauss's tone-poem was no more than background to the illusion even as was Mr. Jones's decoration. In the dim distance was the shadowy portal of a medieval cathedral, as it might be in Til's own Braunschweig. Around it in pure fantasy were topsy-turvy pinnacles of a medieval town, gabled roofs, turrets, chimney pots, dormered windows as cracked and tumbled and out of all normal semblance as the wits and the pranks of Eulenspiegel himself.

So Mr. Jones construes into decoration the ancient folk tale and the modern German tone-poem. Even more fortunately and persuasively has he lavished upon the costumes his wit, fancy, readiness of design, zest for color. Peaked headdresses, comparable in height in their kind with Thamar's tower, were poised upon the heads of the opulent dames of the haute bourgeoisie. Trains of rich stuffs trailed ten yards behind them in the flaunted splendor of "position." The pedantic professors were ludicrous to see in shovel hats that were longer even than Don Basilio's in *The Barber*, with their scrolls of learning tucked under their arms, with their black soutanes billowing to their pompous gait. As black under their peaked caps, with white crosses flaring at their backs, were the Inquisitors, fond and foolish men, who sent Til to the gallows because he mocked at things as they are and upset the precious proprieties. To and fro among the august ladies, the learned, the bench, the rich possessors generally, went the rabble that trailed wondering and elated at the heels of Til. Coarse stuffs, dull colored and rudely caught together, covered them. As often as not back and sides, as in the old ballad, went bare. Greasy were their caps; slovenly was their mien. As night descended upon the "public place" where the action occurred, they were alternately somber figures of shadow or lurid figures of passing gleam. Usually, as the eye looked upon the stage, the illusion was of the swiftly turning pages of a medieval chronicle from the brushes of an illuminator who served equally wit, fancy, and the verities.

That action, more than once enriched or modulated by Mr. Nijinsky's fertile invention, followed in the main the suggestions that the imaginations of men, primed with the fact and the legend of Til, have found in Strauss's tone-poem. The introductory measures set the scene, as it were, with the haute bourgeoisie, descending stately from its mansions; with the rabble streaming up from its alleys. Til opened wide the bread vendor's basket; and the hungry were fed. Til pranced and leered about the highly respectable and highly self-conscious dames with his parodies of courtly coquetry. Til made the professors the mock of their own pedantry. Out of his long mantle, as Mr. Nijinsky swung the folds, peered ever the cloven hoof of his derision. Out of his eyes, in Mr. Nijinsky's astute and graphic miming, shone the elation of him that scores merrily off the truly good. His very steps, as Mr. Nijinsky danced them, were as the tracing of his mockery.

So far Strauss, the attributed program to his rondo, the evergreen traditions of the "merry pranks" that the composer has sent from Bavaria world-wide. Then, for climax, the wry, the comic, the modern rather than medieval, the finely touched and the finely stimulating invention of Mr. Nijinsky himself. Nightfall comes; the respectable are at home and abed; only the rabble, fed, happy, elated, intoxicated with the happenings of Til's afternoon, haunt the square. Regardless of what Strauss's music may or may not imply, heedless of the tradition that the radical Nijinsky has thrown to the winds, they acclaim and enthrone him as their deliverer. On the shoulders of the mob sits Til, enthroned, the sovereign of the wit that brings freedom, of the mockery that sends conventions and hypocrisies toppling down. Respectable Braunschweig and disregarded Strauss may endure no more. Into the "public place" troop the Inquisitors; back to Til's trial and hanging comes the tone-poem. Then and there he is strung up—red light of warning. But no sooner are the executioners gone than he springs anew into being, the perpetual being of the humor that bursts sham, the jeer that pricks pretension. Wistfully, prophetically—to Strauss's epilogue—the rabble eyes a perennial miracle. In fine, a mimodrama—to return to that exceedingly elastic category—like no other in the Russian repertoire; that courts a certain verity of illusion of time, place, and circumstance; yet is impregnated with an everlasting symbolism; that under medieval guise masks intensely contemporary ideas; that takes its text from Strauss's music and from the folk tale of Til and leaves Mr. Nijinsky thereon to preach the sermon; that fills the eye with pictorial illusions; the imagination with thick-coming fancies; the mind with thoughts that twinge. It is the handiwork of an intellect, invention, and fancy that shows Mr. Nijinsky more than the master dancer of his time; that offers a new and fruitful field to mimodrama; it confirms the distinction that marks the Russian Ballet as one of the driving artistic forces of our time. To an eighth art almost, it goes forward.

THE DRAWINGS OF NIJINSKY

BY MARSDEN HARTLEY

READING the book of Romola Nijinsky on Nijinsky and that of Arnold Haskell on Balletomania, one covers pretty much the whole range of dancing up to the time of the present which is the era of Massine and Lifar, and all those other new ones who would doubtless sniff at these, to them, old-fashioned names. It was, I must now suppose, curiosity that led me to see all the great dancers of the last schools, as it was certainly a natural dislike for this sort of expression that permitted me to sniff at the great Isadora, and therefore miss her at her best moments, but such is the case, and I missed out on Isadora.

I saw all the great dancers of the academic past, Pavlova, Karsavina, Fokine, Nijinsky, Bolm, all the way down to the wax-doll perfection of Adeline Genee of whom there is a surprising present-day replica in the appearance of the great skater, Sonia Henie, and there was great charm in Genee, who retired to become the wife of a presumably rich civilian and seems never to have appeared again.

A few years ago Mme. Nijinsky held an exhibition in a new gallery at the top of the Waldorf-Astoria Hotel, and which was chiefly and for obvious reasons a record of the pathological condition of this artist after he had crossed the strange meridian of schizophrenia, and the tragic reaching too far, or was he perhaps driven too far toward the precipice of irrelevant interests, and being peasant, knew nothing of the vast areas into which the mind may be plunged, and left gasping there? Romola Nijinsky records the last conscious states of her husband with a vivid sense of their reality, where in some hall in Switzerland, perhaps at Davos, the dancer was determined to perform the "greatest of all dances," and the title, typical enough for a going mind, the dance of "Le Mariage avec Dieu."

All this sort of thing is pretty much known now and all of us talk of it as glibly as if it had always been everyday language, and while of course the conditions themselves have always been, it is only during the last twenty-five years or so that we have been provided with glib phrases to cover it, even to a recent criticism of the Poems of Mallarmé, where little else than the Freudian was spoken of, more than a little dull, some of us thought, since Mallarmé was a poet to be talked of, as poet. But in the Nijinsky case there is nothing else to do, because the basis of the drawings is entirely created by this condition of split personality, and since both Freud and Jung have seen and commented on these drawings, we would sort of like to know what they said, but I do not seem to recall finding just that in the Romola Nijinsky book.

6 8

A Drawing by Nijinsky. 1919.

But if we take "Le Mariage avec Dieu" to begin with, we shall see the whole thing in these drawings as they progress from stage to stage, from the vague and useless beginnings where curved lines are used to the point of monotony, and the figure of the female appears, no vital contact with the female principle being remarked. It is not the expression of a male thinking solely and passionately about the female or a female, as it is hardly likely what Nijinsky was to be doing, for he was by nature an abstract artist, even though he was not an intellectual one.

At all events, these drawings are psychopathic charts and that is all that can be said of them, for they are almost entirely without merit, that is to say esthetic merit. They are not creations of the vibrant living imagination; they are records of a mind wandering through the corridors of the where to the black abysses of the nowhere.

And these drawings are singular and entertainingly innocent; for since Nijinsky must have been just a natural clean little boy, he didn't get caught up with decadent symbols, and of this there is absolutely nothing in these drawings of his.

It is as if no record at all were made of the period previous to his meeting with Diaghilev, so that the first series of drawings are of the rhythms of the feminine idea, and the last two are the black pantherlike spirit that pursued him and plunged him over the precipice of knowing all to knowing nothing.

There is no doubt whatever but that Diaghilev was the creator of Nijinsky as he was of all the others that came into contact with him and enlisted or aroused his interests. He could look at them and in the instant know what sort of a dancer he could or would make of them, and if the imagination of Diaghilev was dark-ghoulish, as why shouldn't it be thought of that way, since he felt the need of expressing glory and luxury on such vast scales, he was "dark" himself, and sought the excitement of the artifices for his light.

These drawings of Nijinsky are free of all the common forms of pornographic indulgence. There is no trace that this sort of thing ever played a role in his consciousness, certainly not from the drawings.

And if the demon in pursuit which figures as the fearful design in the last two series of drawings is far more powerful than the attempt to find out the place of the feminine principle in his nature, it is because when the mind, being driven to desperation by his attempts to fulfill the common offices of life, began to break, it is perfectly natural that the image in the drawing should be that of the image that attempted to destroy him, and what other image could that be, but that of the one who had put the halo of glory about his being, and set him among the clouds that were burning with sunset fire—who could that have been save the thing he feared in Diaghilev, if not, let's say for decency's sake, Diaghilev himself?

The great Russian ballet director was a powerful hypnotist. He was something of a performer of the occult trick; he took handfuls of diamonds out of coal pockets; he took rubies out of pools of blood, he took sapphires out of the crowded places among the constellations, he took black out of despair,

Water color by Nijinsky. 1922.

red out of the body of physical lusts; and if he took white to any extent, he had to have plenty of the corroding rays of the moon upon it. The very look of Diaghilev's own eye in a common photo shows that he played with fires of which he was in one way no master, and in another way with which he played too much and too dangerously.

Black magic is one of the elements of everyday life, and gods help the individual and I am not putting on the occult "dog" here because I know almost nothing at all about it, but it is the language of these drawings of Nijinsky and by the drawings alone one can easily frame a perfect sense of the last conscious image in Nijinsky's mind before the split, and it is perfectly natural that it should be God. It was a kind of primitive offering on the part of the dancer in this case, to identify himself with the maker of his pitiable dreams.

And it is not the eye of God that appears in the drawings one after another, in the latter series; it is the eye of the dreaded pursuing demon, and all obviously has to do with the instant of the entrance of woman into the dancer's life, and the rage in the forest of the demon whose nostrils were spitting sulphuric fires.

The later drawings are in a sort of sticky water color and have for the moment more life, and it swings me back once again to the more direct and vital image that was living in the brain at the time of the disintegration, and it was not the woman who was the great symbol.

These drawings of the last period are mostly in ink and the white of the paper, and here are the beginnings of the two principles at war, and the third which is so telling is the spot of red which appears, which is like the blood spitting of some enraged and outraged demon.

Then the red spot disappears, and the struggle is over, and it is as if you see the eye of the mind closing as you watch, and it is an eye in each case, and in each last drawing the eye seems to grow tighter and tighter, and then the vision is sealed, nothing more is seen.

There is no such vast drama in this life as was involved in the case of Van Gogh, and no such esthetic burning, for the mental problem is entirely different, and in a sense Nijinsky was more fortunate; for Van Gogh's tragic suffering lay in the fact that he was obliged to vacillate between states of clarity and states of sheer insanity, and he himself could not know when the attack would come, all the more distracting since he knew when the states were coming on, he could tell his doctors just what was to happen and seem to follow the condition sort of half sanely even while he was progressing toward insanity, so that the suffering in the soul was infinitely greater, for at least Nijinsky was totally oblivious to all that side of things and was therefore freed of the misery.

Only yesterday in the morning paper we read that Nijinsky is well on the way to a possible recovery, that he is able to drive his car around the park where he is, and seems otherwise on the way toward rationality, but a condition is made—he seems to think that the war is still going on, and Walter Winchell's flip remark in the morning paper is extremely apropos: "After all, what a sane man."

If Nijinsky comes really out of his mental dilemma, it would be interesting to know just what he is able to make of the past, if he can recall where he left off, if he can record some of the stages during the past years and of what they meant to him, or is he to begin like a child again, as if he has just been born, in which case what sort of infantilism will it be? At all events, the drawings of Nijinsky are essentially psychopathic in their value, and are romantic charts merely of the closing down of his mind.

Nijinsky and his wife in his car. London, February, 1917.

Nijinsky backstage after performance of *Petrouchka*, with Karsavina and Diaghilev. Lipnitzki, Paris, 1927.

NOTE ON NIJINSKY LETTER

I WOULD not see Nijinsky again. At the beginning of June, absent from Paris, I wrote him inviting him to hear *Parsifal* with me, the première of which was to take place several days later at the Théâtre des Champs-Elysées. But he received my letter in Madrid, from where he would leave for Vienna with the Ballets Russes. Then came the general dispersion. During the war we exchanged several letters, and here is the last that I received from him, in 1918. I transcribe it textually, to show to what a degree Nijinsky, by pure will power, had perfected himself in the French language—he who had not known a single word when he arrived for the first time in Paris (1909), where he never stayed longer than two or three months at most, and where he spoke all day in Russian with the people of his entourage.

LETTER FROM NIJINSKY
TO REYNALDO HAHN

I WAS very happy to get your news and to learn that you are behaving yourself, and haven't forgotten me. . . . During all these past years I have kept my friendship for you. Your artistic projects and your ideas for ballets interest me very much; I hope soon I may really get to understand them. I work, I compose new dances, and I am perfecting the system of dance-notation, which I have invented in these last years. I am very happy to have found this notation, which for centuries has been searched for, because I believe, and I am sure, my dear friend, you will agree, that this notation is indispensable for the development of the art of the dance. It is a simple and logical means to note down movements. In a word, this system will provide the same service for the artists of the dance that musical notes give to musicians. I shall be very happy to show it to you, and learn your opinion of this work.

I never got the letter which you sent me two years ago. You doubtless know I was interned for eighteen months, with my family in Austria-Hungary. [As a Russian citizen, Nijinsky was considered an enemy alien, although married to a Hungarian.] We passed through many privations and difficulties. After that we went to North America, where I danced. At present, I am living here [St. Moritz, Switzerland] in order to compose a program quietly. I wish to work independently of other troupes of dancers, in which intrigue prevents the creation of real art. I am planning to dance alone with a small company and achieve some interesting results.

I hope that you will have everything to make you happy, I remain your devoted friend,

VASLAV NIJINSKY

(*Figaro*, April 6, 1939.)

VASLAV NIJINSKY BIBLIOGRAPHY
1910-1945

BARBIER, GEORGES. Designs on the dances of Vaslaw Nijinsky. Foreword by Francis Miomandre. Translated by C. W. Beaumont. London, C. W. Beaumont, 1913. 38 pp. plates.

BEAUMONT, CYRIL W. Complete book of ballets. A guide to the principal ballets of the nineteenth and twentieth centuries. London, Putnam & Co., Ltd., 1937. (Vaslav Nijinsky, pp. 790–801.)

BEAUMONT, CYRIL W. Vaslaw Nijinsky. London, C. W. Beaumont, 1932. 28 pp.

BOURMAN, ANATOLE. The tragedy of Nijinsky. By Anatole Bourman in collaboration with D. Lyman. New York, Whittlesey House (McGraw-Hill Book Company, Inc.), 1936. 291 pp. illus. (London edition published by R. Hale, 1937.)

COLUM, MARY M. Nijinsky: art and mental unbalance. *In* Forum. Vol. 97, pp. 161–162. March, 1937.

DOLIN, ANTON. Ballet go round. London, M. Joseph, 1938. (Nijinsky, pp. 238–245.)

The FAUN that has startled Paris. *In* Current Literature, No. 53, pp. 208–210. August, 1912.

FODOR, NANDOR. The riddle of Nijinsky. *In* Dancing Times, pp. 268–269. London, June, 1938.

GATTI, GUIDO M. Il mito di Nijinsky. *In* Pan. Ano 2, pp. 567–575. Milano, 1934.

HARTLEY, MARSDEN. The spangles of existence; casual dissertations, by Marsden Hartley. (Typescript mss; in library of Museum of Modern Art.) (The drawings of Nijinsky, pp. 150–152.)

HASKELL, ARNOLD L. Diaghileff, his artistic and private life. By Arnold L. Haskell in collaboration with Walter Nouvel. New York, Simon and Schuster, Inc., 1935. (Chapter 12. Diaghileff and Nijinsky: fact and fiction.)

KIRSTEIN, LINCOLN. Dance. G. P. Putnam's Sons, 1935. (Nijinsky, pp. 282–293.)

LIFAR, SERGE. Serge Diaghilev; his life, his work, his legend. An intimate biography. New York, G. P. Putnam's Sons, 1940. (Vaslav Nijinsky, pp. 143–150.)

LIFAR, SERGE. Nijinsky revisited. *In* Living Age. Vol. 356, pp. 540–543. New York, August, 1939.

LIFAR, SERGE. Visit to the insane asylum and its reactions on Nijinsky. *In* Life. Vol. 7, pp. 22–23. New York, July 3, 1939.

MARTIN, JOHN. Introduction to the dance. New York, W. W. Norton & Company, Inc., 1939. (Nijinsky and Diaghilev, pp. 196–203.)

MOLINEAU, JANE. Nijinsky—artist and man. *In* Bellman. Vol. 21, pp. 822–827. Minneapolis, 1916.

MONTENEGRO, ROBERT. Vaslaw Nijinsky; an artistic interpretation of his work in black, and white and gold; with a note of introduction by C. W. Beaumont. London, C. W. Beaumont, 1913. iv + 10 plates.

MOORE, LILLIAN. Artists of the dance. New York, The Thomas Y. Crowell Company, 1938. (Vaslav Nijinsky, pp. 193–202.)

MULLOCK, DOROTHY. Seven wood-cuts of Nijinsky, the Russian danseur. (London, Sapphire Press, n.d.) 7 mounted plates.

NIJINSKY, ROMOLA. Nijinsky, by Romola Nijinsky. Foreword by Paul Claudel. New York, Simon and Schuster, Inc., 1934. xvii + 435 pp. illus. London edition, published by V. Gollancz, 1933. Budapest edition, published by Nyugat, 1935.

NIJINSKY, VASLAV. The diary of Vaslav Nijinsky. Edited by Romola Nijinsky. New York, Simon and Schuster, Inc., 1936. 187 pp. illus.

NIJINSKY, VASLAW. How I conceive my roles. In Musical Courier. Vol. 73, pp. 40–41. New York, December, 1916.

NIJINSKY, VASLAV. Six vers de Jean Cocteau. Six dessins de Paul Iribe. Paris, Société Général d'Impression, n.d. 12 pp.

NIJINSKY-MARKEVITCH, KYRA. Nijinsky et la legende. In Suisse romande. Vol. 3, pp. 114–117. Lausanne, 1939.

PROPERT, WALTER A. The Russian Ballet in Western Europe, 1909–1920; with a chapter on the music by Eugene Goossens. London, John Lane, Ltd., 1921. (Nijinsky, pp. 75–84.)

READ, HERBERT. The Group Theatre presents an exhibition of drawings, water colours and pastels by Nijinsky . . . Foreword by Herbert Read. London, The Storran Gallery, 1937. 16 pp. plates.

ROBERTS, MARY FANTON. Nijinsky, the great Russian: his art and his personality. In Craftsman. Vol. 31, pp. 52–64. New York, 1916.

SCHNACK, ANTON. Nijinsky sitzt in der Oper. In Reclams universum. Jahrg. 46, pp. 412–413. Leipzig, February 13, 1930.

SVETLOV, VALERIAN. Will Nijinsky dance again? In Dance magazine. Vol. 12, pp. 18 ff. New York, May, 1929.

TYLER, PARKER. I see the pattern of Nijinsky clear. In View. Ser. 5, no. 4, pp. 4–5. New York, November, 1945.

WALTON, WILLIAM. Nijinsky in Vienna: the man who was once world's greatest dancer has come out of the war alive but still mad. In Life. Vol. 19, pp. 63–64. New York, September 10, 1945.

WHITWORTH, GEOFFREY. The art of Nijinsky; with ten illustrations by Dorothy Mullock. London, Chatto & Windus, 1913. ix + 109 pp. illus.

WILENTZ, LILLIAN. Nijinsky: transition from the ballet. In Dance Observer. Vol. 5, pp. 22–23. New York, February, 1938.

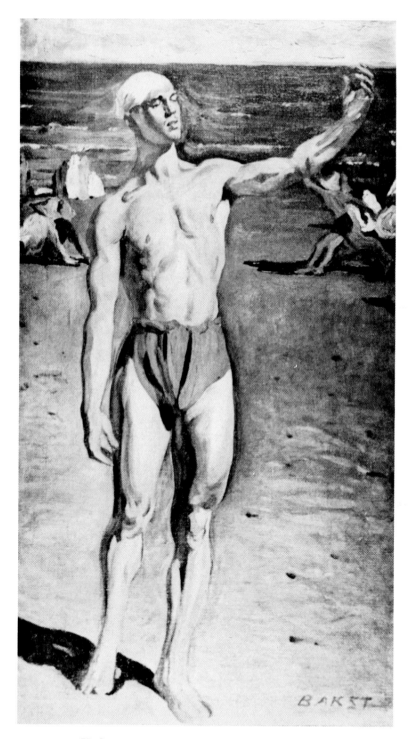

Vaslav Nijinsky. Portrait by Leon Bakst. ca. 1909.

L'APRES-MIDI D'UN FAUNE. Book: Vaslav Nijinsky. Music: Claude Debussy. Scenery and Costumes: Léon Bakst. Choreography: Vaslav Nijinsky. First produced: Théâtre du Châtelet, Paris, May 29, 1912.

LE SACRE DU PRINTEMPS. Book: Igor Stravinsky and Nicholas Roerich. Music: Igor Stravinsky. Scenery and Costumes: Nicholas Roerich. Choreography: Vaslav Nijinsky. First produced: Théâtre des Champs-Elysées, Paris, May 29, 1913.

JEUX. Book: Vaslav Nijinsky. Music: Claude Debussy. Scenery and Costumes: Léon Bakst. Choreography: Vaslav Nijinsky. First produced: Théâtre des Champs-Elysées, Paris, May 15, 1913.

TIL EULENSPIEGEL. Book: Vaslav Nijinsky. Music: Richard Strauss. Scenery and Costumes: Robert Edmond Jones. Choreography: Vaslav Nijinsky. First produced: Manhattan Opera House, New York, October 23, 1916.

Vaslav Nijinsky by John Singer Sargent. London, 1913.

PAVLOVA

Anna Pavlova. St. Petersburg, 1906.

PREFACE

OVER fifteen years have passed since the miracle of Anna Pavlova's dancing finally came to an end, but the heritage of this great artist is still a moving force in the dance today.

She appeared on most of the stages of the world, leaving the memory of her art in the great theaters of the largest cities and in the small towns. Pavlova performed with most of the great dancers of our time—Mordkin, Novikoff, and Volinine of the Imperial Ballet of Moscow; Fokine, Bolm, Nijinsky, and Vladimiroff of her own St. Petersburg Academy. As a performer she benefited little from the progress in the technical arts of the theater, appearing in clumsily produced, badly mounted and designed ballets, which were undistinguished by any artistic contribution save her own. But so shining and ineluctable was her genius that when she danced, one was conscious of nothing but the emotion which she seemed uniquely to create. Pavlova could accept without hesitation the vaudeville and music-hall bookings which frequently forced her to compete on the same bill with a trained seal or a cockney monologist, so great was her personal dignity and so instant and stilling her presence on a stage. No artist, not even the immortal Sarah Bernhardt, knew such universal homage as Pavlova, from the time of her debut to the day of her death. Few so richly deserved it.

Today, the lasting influence of this great woman and the timeless recollection of her magnificent art make it seem more, rather than less, of a miracle that Anna Pavlova once lived and danced.

In this Ballet Society monograph on Anna Pavlova, Carl Van Vechten has contributed a nostalgic view of the great dancer. He is still one of our most fascinating critics, and his faithful attendance at major dance events for more than a third of a century has contributed enormously to our appreciation of this art. It is regrettable that his current observations are not published now, for his reviews, written long ago, could serve today as a model of dance criticism. Carl Van Vechten is much like his nineteenth century predecessor, Théophile Gautier, at once storyteller, belle-lettrist and the major dance critic of his time.

The pictures selected for this book are typical of the photographer's art of the first part of this century. They are sometimes excellent, often ordinary, occasionally communicative; and yet, taken all together, reflect but a fragment of the Pavlova image. Marianne Moore has invested these photographs with her own insight; thus, she has given them a particular meaning and made possible for us

a more vivid, touching and poetic understanding. Through her own artistry, we can see more clearly defined the magic of another artist. This is not enough—it never is—but it is all that we can have and it impels our imagination to supply the rest.

For dancing is the most elusive of all the stage arts—fleeting and gone, until the next performance. When a dancer passes from the stage, there are left the programs, press notices and photographs. No matter how artfully put together, these remains can barely do more than evoke the melancholy wish that one should have seen more—and looked harder.

CONTENTS

Pavlova in *The Dying Swan*. New York. Mishkin, 1914.

PAVLOVA DEAD

Pavlova, will you dance no more?
Will the tulip shut up in the earth?
Will the swan forever fold white wings?
Will the flute go silent
And the song be hushed in the air?
Will the ray full of rainbows flicker and fail?

Pavlova, your foot is lighter than the perfume of lilies

Brighter than the sparkle of waves,
More musical than the thrush at twilight.
Somewhere—oh, softly—

Pavlova, will you dance no more?

HARRIET MONROE

From *Chosen Poems* by Harriet Monroe. By
permission of The Macmillan Company, publishers.

PAVLOVA

ANNA PAVLOVA: PAGES OF MY LIFE

VIVID are my earliest recollections, which take me back to the time when I was living in a little flat with my mother at Petrograd. I was the only child; and my father having died two years after my birth, we two were alone in the world.

My mother was a most pious woman. She taught me to cross myself and pray in front of the holy ikon in our sitting room. The Blessed Virgin, whose sweet wistful eyes seemed to look kindly into mine, became a beloved friend. I used to hold conversations with her every morning and every evening, telling her all my infant woes, all my little joys and hopes.

We were poor—very poor indeed; and yet my mother would never fail to provide, on the occasion of feast days, a surprise for me, in the shape of some treat. For instance, at Easter, I would discover with glee some pretty toys enclosed in a gigantic egg. At Christmas we always had our Christmas tree, a little fir adorned with golden fruit shimmering with the reflected light of many little candles. And I can still remember my enthusiasm when one day (I was eight years old) I heard that we were to celebrate Christmas by going to see a performance at the Marinsky Theater.

I had never yet been to the theater, and I plied my mother with questions in order to find out what kind of show it was that we were going to see. She replied by telling me the story of the Sleeping Beauty—a favorite of mine among all fairy tales, and one which she had already told me countless times.

When we started for the Marinsky Theater, the snow was brightly shining in the reflected light of street lamps and shop windows. Our sleigh was

1

noiselessly speeding along the hard surface, and I felt unspeakably happy, seated beside my mother, her arm tenderly enclosing my waist. "You are going to enter fairyland," said she, as we were being whirled across the darkness toward the theater, that mysterious unknown.

THE FIRST CALL OF THE VOCATION

The music of the "Sleeping Beauty" is by our great Chaikovsky. As soon as the orchestra began to play, I became very grave and attentive, eagerly listening, moved for the first time in my life by the call of Beauty. But when the curtain rose, displaying the golden hall of a wonderful palace, I could not withhold a shout of delight. And I remember hiding my face in my hands when the old hag appeared on the stage in her car driven by rats.

In the second act a swarm of youths and maidens appeared, and danced a most delightful waltz.

—"How would you like to dance thus?" asked my mother with a smile.

—"Oh," I replied, "I should prefer to dance as the pretty lady does who plays the part of the Princess. One day I shall be the Princess, and dance upon the stage of this very theater."

My mother muttered that I was her silly little dear, and never suspected that I had just discovered the idea that was to guide me throughout my life.

When we left the theater, I was living in a dream. During the journey home, I kept thinking of the day when I should make my first appearance on the stage, in the part of the Sleeping Beauty.

—"Darling mother," I said as soon as we had reached home, "you will have me taught to dance, won't you?"

—"Yes, certainly, my little Nura (that was her pet name for me), I shall," she replied, kissing me, and no doubt thinking of the joy she would experience in seeing me waltz at the time when, having reached a marriageable age, I should be taken out into society.

But it was not of society nor of ballrooms that I was dreaming. All my thoughts were centered on the ballet. That very night, I dreamed that I was a ballerina, and spent my whole life dancing, like a butterfly, to the sounds of Chaikovsky's lovely music. I love to remember that night, which was to be the prime mover of my career, with all the joys and pains which it was to bring me.

The next morning I could speak of nought but of my great resolve. Then my mother began to understand that her daughter was a most earnest and determined little person.

—"In order to become a dancer," she said, "you will have to leave your mother and become a pupil of the Ballet School. My little Nura would not like to forsake her mamma, would she? Most certainly not!"

—"No," I replied, "I have no wish to leave you, Mamma dear. But if it is necessary for me to part with you in order to become a Ballerina, I shall have to resign myself to it." And, kissing her, I begged her to secure my admission to the school.

She refused, and I began to weep. It was only a few days later, wondering at my firmness of purpose, that she complied with my desire, and took me to see the director of the school.

We were, as I said, extremely poor. And it was perhaps in the hope of providing for me at a time when she would no longer be with me, and when I should have to make my way alone and unassisted, that she decided upon

that interview—no doubt a great sacrifice on her part.

—"The regulations do not allow us to admit eight-year-old children," the director said. "Bring her back when she will have completed her tenth year."

And so I had two years to wait—two years during which I remained sad and dreamy, haunted as I was by the desire to become a Ballerina as soon as possible.

I ENTER THE BALLET SCHOOL

According to the custom of those who live in Petrograd, we used to spend our summers in the country, not far from town. It was always a pleasure for me to see our belongings, chairs and tables and beds and crockery and kitchen implements (not forgetting the big samovar) packed in a van and carried to the *dacha,* the wooden cottage no bigger than a doll's house. In Russia, when one is in the country, one is allowed to live according to one's fancy. And we elected to spend practically the whole of our days on our veranda. It is there we took our meals; and there my mother used to make me

Caricature of Pavlova by Nicholas Legat. St. Petersburg, 1904.

read Kyrlof's Fables aloud, or teach me to sew.

Bareheaded, and clad in an old cotton frock, I often would explore the woods close by the cottage. I enjoyed the mysterious aspect of the cloister-like alleys under the fir trees, all peopled with dancing butterflies. I sought out the most secluded spots, and would sit under a shady tree to build in the air the fragile castles of my dreams.

At times I wove myself a wreath of wild flowers, and imagined myself to be the Beauty asleep in her enchanted castle.

On my tenth birthday I told my mother that the time had come again to call on the director of the school. She looked very grave, but did as I had asked her.

I shall not attempt to describe my rapture when the director promised to secure my admittance to the school. Nevertheless, I shed tears when the day came upon which I had to take leave of my mother. She too wept. I did not understand the reason for her tears, as I understand it now. I was relinquishing the happy peaceful life of home, under the protection of the silver Virgin, and entering the very trying, intoxicating life of a widely different world, the world of art and of

the stage. She realized that there could be henceforth no turning back, and that was why she felt sad; for, although one may fail to find happiness in theatrical life, one never wishes to give it up after having once tasted its fruits.

To enter the School of the Imperial Ballet is to enter a convent whence frivolity is banned, and where merciless discipline reigns.

Every morning at eight, the solemn tolling of a big bell would put an end to our sleep. We dressed under the stern eyes of a governess, whose duty it was to see that all hands were kept perfectly clean, all nails in good trim, and all teeth carefully washed. When we were ready, we went to prayers, which were sung by one of the older pupils in front of an ikon underneath which a tiny flickering lamp was burning like a little red star. At nine, breakfast—tea, bread and butter—was served, and immediately afterward the dancing lesson began.

We were all gathered in a big room, very high and well lit. There was no furniture except a few benches, a piano, and enormous mirrors. The walls were decorated with portraits of Russia's sovereigns. After the small novices' lesson, the elder, more advanced pupils

5

had their turn, and the beginners withdrew to another room, where they pursued their work.

At twelve the bell rang for lunch, after which we were taken out for a walk. Then more exercises until four o'clock, and then dinner. After dinner we enjoyed a period of leisure. Then came fencing lessons, music lessons, and from time to time rehearsals of dances, which were to be performed on the stage of the Marinsky Theater. When we children had to appear in a ballet, we were taken to the theater in great, well-closed cars. Supper used to be at eight, and an hour later we were sent to bed. On feast days we were taken to one of the Imperial Theaters: at times to the Theater Michel, to see French plays performed by the French artists belonging to the Imperial company.

The most exciting days in our well-ordered life were those when the Emperor paid a visit to the school. In those times the imperial family used to mark their interest in the school by frequent visits. And then, to please the Empress, the children would perform a ballet on the school's little stage.

I can remember that one day, when I was a little girl, the Emperor Alexander and the Empress Maria, with other members of the imperial family, came to see one of those performances. At the end of the ballet we were allowed to go into the auditorium. The Tsar took my little comrade, Stanislava Belinskaya, in his arms. He was so kind-hearted and unaffected, in all respects a true Russian! At that very instant I burst into tears. Naturally I was asked why I wept. And between two sobs I replied, with tears trickling fast down my cheeks: "I want the Emperor to take me into his arms too!" Grand Duke Vladimir, in order to comfort me, took me upon his knee. But I was not satisfied, and went on weeping and repeating, "I want the Emperor to kiss me!" The Grand Duke laughed heartily.

After the performance, the imperial family would come to the dining room and have tea with us. We were not in the least embarrassed by their presence. The Emperor and Empress were so kind, so very much like a kind father and mother, that we were quite at ease with them, and altogether content.

Every Sunday my mother came to see me; and I used to spend all my holidays with her. During the summer we always lived in the country. We grew so fond of our little holiday cot-

Top: Pavlova as a student at Imperial Ballet School. Bottom: Pavlova in *The Sleeping Beauty*. St. Petersburg, ca. 1906.

tage, that even now we have not the heart to give it up in favor of some more comfortable abode. And I am writing these pages upon a table on the veranda, amidst surroundings which I love because every feature reminds me of the days of my childhood.

I BECOME "PREMIERE DANSEUSE"

I left the Ballet School at the age of sixteen; and shortly afterward I was permitted to style myself "Première Danseuse"—which is an official title, exactly as that of "*tchinovnik*" in government offices. Later I was granted the title of Ballerina, which only four other dancers of the present time have received.

After reading Taglioni's life, I conceived the notion of dancing in foreign countries—for the celebrated Italian used to appear everywhere. She danced at Paris, at London, and in Russia, where she is still remembered. A cast of her little foot is preserved at Petrograd.

One of the first exercises which the would-be dancer has to perform is to stand on tiptoe. At first, the child can hardly remain in that position for more than a second: but methodical training gradually strengthens the muscles of her toes, so that after a time she is able to make a few steps—clumsily at first, and very much after the fashion of a tyro skater; then, in proportion as she acquires proficiency, the little dancer learns to walk on tiptoe as easily as a violinist performs a scale on his instrument.

After having mastered that first difficulty, the pupil has to get acquainted with steps of all kinds. The teacher performs a few steps; then half a dozen children imitate his movements as best they can for ten minutes, while the others watch. Then the little performers are allowed to rest, and others take their place. Apart from numerous, varied, and complicated steps which belong to the classical ballet, one has to learn a number of national and historical dances; the minuet, the mazurka, Hungarian, Italian, Spanish dances, and so forth.

As is the case in all branches of art, success depends in a very large measure upon individual initiative and exertion, and cannot be achieved except by dint of hard work. Even after having reached perfection, a Ballerina may never indulge in idleness. If she wishes to preserve what she has acquired, she must practice her exercises every day, exactly as the pianist has to practice his scales. For the dancer must feel so perfectly at ease so far as technique is concerned, that when on the stage she need devote to it not a single thought, and may concentrate upon expression, upon the feelings which must give life to the dances she is performing.

Equal care must be devoted to acquiring the art of dancing with a partner, which is something quite special and apart. The Ballerina must learn how to assume graceful postures in endless variety, to avoid conveying an impression of monotony which would induce weariness: for instance, when after each of her pirouettes her partner catches her in his arms. All this again calls for constant practice and no small variety of exercises.

At the School of the Imperial Ballet the history of the art of dancing is now included in the curriculum, and is one of the matters set for the yearly examinations. The art of making up is taught with very special care and thoroughness; for a dancer is naturally expected to be capable of appearing at will as a Spanish maiden, or Chinese, or Greek, not to mention dozens of other types.

My first tour began with Riga, in 1907. That town, with its winding streets and its Gothic buildings, is German, not Russian. I arrived with a company, and we performed two ballets at the opera house.

The good Germans of Riga welcomed us so warmly that I felt encouraged to extend the scope of my tour. So from Riga we went to Helsingfors, Stockholm, Copenhagen, Prague, and Berlin. Everywhere our dancing was hailed as the revelation of an art so far unknown.

At Stockholm, King Oscar attended our show every evening, which of course gratified me highly. Nevertheless, I was deeply surprised when one day a chamberlain came to inform me that the King wished to see me at the palace. One of the royal carriages was sent for me, and I drove through the streets of the capital as if I were a real princess. The King received me in an immense room which I had already seen when visiting, as all tourists do, the royal palace. He made a little speech, very kind and charming, to thank me for the pleasure which my dancing had given him. He also granted me the emblem of the Swedish order "Litteris et Artibus." He told me that he liked the dances of southern Europe above all things; and that of all the dances that he had seen me per-

Pavlova with her husband, Victor Dandré. London, 1912.

form, it was a Spanish one that he preferred.

I fully appreciated the Sovereign's most flattering graciousness; but I was even more deeply delighted by the spontaneous tribute of the big crowd that one night assembled, and paid me the compliment of escorting me from the theater to the hotel.

There are people who refuse to believe that a dancer's life can be otherwise than frivolous. But, in fact, the dancer's profession is altogether incompatible with a frivolous mode of living. If a dancer, yielding to temptation, ceases to exercise over herself the strictest control, she will find it impossible to continue dancing. She must sacrifice herself to her art. Her reward will be the power to help those who come to see her to forget awhile the sadnesses and monotony of life.

10

That much I realized, for the first time, at Stockholm.

In the crowd which escorted me when I left the theater, there were people of all stations: men and women belonging to the middle-class bourgeoisie, clerks and workmen, dressmakers' hands, shop assistants. They were all following my car, silently, and then remained standing in front of my hotel until I was told that they wished me to show myself on the balcony. As soon as they saw me, they greeted me with a stormy outburst of cheers which, coming after the deep protracted silence, sounded almost alarming. I bowed my head to them from time to time; and all of a sudden they started singing national tunes in my honor. I stood vainly seeking for a way of expressing my gratefulness to them. Then an idea struck me. I turned into my room, and came back with the wreaths and baskets of flowers which had been handed to me on the stage. But even after I had thrown roses and lilies and violets and lilacs to the crowd, they seemed loath to retire. I was deeply moved and quite embarrassed. I could not help asking my maid, "But what have I done to move them to so great an enthusiasm?"

"Madam," she replied, "you have made them happy by enabling them to forget for an hour the sadnesses of life."

I never forgot those words. By speaking thus, my maid, a simple Russian peasant girl, gave me a new goal for my art.

MY TOUR THROUGH AMERICA

The following year I went with a Russian company to Leipzig, Prague, and Vienna. We were dancing Chaikovsky's beautiful "The Swans' Lake." Later I joined Mr. Diaghilev's company, in order to show Paris the art of the Russian Ballet. Mr. Fokine, the ballet master, succeeded in pleasing the Parisians, who have so refined and so critical an understanding of art. He is a man of genius; and I am delighted that he should have succeeded at Covent Garden too.

Yet, the beauty of the scenes he combines, the splendors of the setting and costumes, the charm of the music, exercise so captivating and surprising an effect upon the public, that the dancer's individuality is lost sight of. Therefore Paris, whilst acquainted with the Russian Ballet in the form given to it abroad by Fokine's genius, does not

11

Pavlova in *La Bayadere*. St. Petersburg, ca. 1906.

know me as England and America do.

During the course of that season in Paris, I crossed the Channel in order to dance at a reception given by Lady Londersborough in honor of King Edward and Queen Alexandra. Their Majesties were graciously pleased to express their thanks for the pleasure which they had taken in my dances.

I returned to London in 1910, in order to appear at the Palace Theater. Several friends had warned me that a first-class dancer belonging to the Imperial Ballet should not appear on the stage of a music hall. But I knew the London public and the London theaters so well, that not for one instant did I hesitate to sign a contract binding me to appear at the Palace. And I never had cause to regret having signed it.

The British public is most kind and sensitive. It has always been a great joy for me to find that British audiences evince a marked preference for the very dances I like best, and in which I give the utmost and best that is in me. I have the feeling now that perfect understanding exists between the British public and myself.

A tour to America, in the course of which I danced at the Metropolitan Opera, New York, followed by a Lon-

don season. Naturally, I was delighted with the welcome I found in that country. The newspapers published portraits of me, essays on my art, interviews, and, to tell the whole truth, yarns of all kinds concerning my life, my tastes, my ideas. I have had many a good laugh reading those extraordinary fanciful articles, and discovering in them that I am the strangest and queerest person in the whole world. The American journalist may indeed be proud of his marvelous imagination.

After New York, our tour carried us through various states. It was a triumphal march, but an exceedingly fatiguing one. We lived in the special train which was taking us from one place to another across thousands of miles of country. Sometimes we would arrive at a certain spot with just time enough to go from the train to the theater for the performance. Hardly did the performance end before we rushed posthaste back to the train, which whirled us away throughout the night (and perhaps the following day as well) toward some other town where a performance was due. It was desired that I should return to America the following year, and I longed to do so; but I lacked the physical energy to repeat so arduous a journey across the new continent. The ordeal is far too trying to the nerves.

We stayed at little towns in Canada: at Vancouver among other places. An incident which took place there, though trifling, amused me greatly; it illustrates the delightful courtesy of the Canadians.

After having danced at the theater, I wished to go and have some supper at a restaurant. I found every table occupied, and not one seat vacant. Several people, having recognized me, offered their seats to me; and I was feeling so tired that in the end I accepted one. When I had finished my meal, a gentleman who was seated at another table stood up, and in an ex-temporized speech asked all present to drink my health.

His kind attention pleased me greatly. But I remember that my chief concern was for the old traveling suit which I was wearing—I am not ashamed to acknowledge as much: any woman would have felt the same under similar circumstances. But my old clothes did not stand me in bad stead: all responded to the invitation, and drained their glasses in my honor.

The next day, the incident was described in the newspapers. The Americans, eager not to be outdone in the matter of courtesy, paid me a similar compliment at Portland.

Pavlova with her swans at Ivy House, London, in costume of *Russian Dance*, ca. 1912.

ART, THE SOLE MASTER OF MY LIFE

I have spoken so much about myself, that I think I may continue awhile, in order to reply to a question which is often made to me. In my opinion a true artist must devote herself wholly to her art. She has no right to lead the life that most women long for.

. . . The wind rustles through the branches of the fir trees in the forest opposite my veranda, the forest through which, as a child, I longed to rove. The stars shine in the evening gloom. I have come to the end of these few recollections. While writing them down, I started realizing more fully the purpose of my life and its unity. To tend, unfailingly, unflinchingly, toward a goal, is the secret of success. But success? What exactly is success? For me it is to be found not in applause, but in the satisfaction of feeling that one is realizing one's ideal. When, a small child, I was rambling over there by the fir trees, I thought that success spelled happiness.

I was wrong. Happiness is like a butterfly which appears and delights us for one brief moment, but soon flits away.

Translated by Sebastien Voirol

Pavlova in her parlor at Ivy House. London, 1912.

PAVLOVA AT THE METROPOLITAN OPERA HOUSE

by CARL VAN VECHTEN

MORE than two-thirds of the boxes at the Metropolitan Opera House were still filled with their occupants at half after 12 last night. It was not a performance of *Götterdämmerung* without cuts that kept a fashionable audience in its seats, but the American debut of Anna Pavlova, the Russian dancer from the Imperial Opera in St. Petersburg. Mme. Pavlova appeared in a revival of *Coppélia,* which was given at the Metropolitan for the first time since the season of 1904-5. As this was preceded by a performance by *Werther,* the ballet did not commence until after 11, and it was nearly 1 before it was finished.

However, Mme. Pavlova easily held most of her audience. It is safe to say that such dancing has not been seen on the local stage during the present generation. If Pavlova were a regular member of the Metropolitan Opera Company it would also be safe to prophesy a revival of favor for the classic ballet.

The little dancer is lithe and exquisitely formed. When she first appeared just after the curtain rose, there was a dead silence. She received no welcome. She wore the conventional ballet dress and her dark hair was bound back with a blue band.

After the first waltz, which immediately follows her entrance, the audience burst into vociferous applause, which was thereafter repeated at every possible opportunity. Pavlova received an ovation of the sort that is seldom given to anybody at the theater.

And her dancing deserved it. To begin with, her technique is of a sort

Opposite page, top: Pavlova in *Pavillon D'Armide* and *Don Quixote.* Bottom left: *California Poppy.* Bottom right: *La Fille Mal Gardée.*

17

to dazzle the eye. The most difficult tricks of the art of the dancer she executed with supreme ease. She even went further. There were gasps of astonishment and bursts of applause after several of her remarkable feats, all of which were accomplished with the greatest ease and lightness.

Grace, a certain sensuous charm, and a decided sense of humor are other qualities which she possesses. In fact, it would be difficult to conceive a dancer who so nearly realizes the ideal of this sort of dancing.

In the first act she was assisted at times by Mikhail Mordkin, who also comes from St. Petersburg, and who is only second to Pavlova as a remarkable dancer. Their *pas de deux* near the end of the act was perhaps the best liked bit of the evening. It was in the second act in her impersonation of the doll that Pavlova disclosed her charming sense of humor.

At this time it is impossible to write any more about this dancer, but there is no doubt that she will prove a great attraction while she remains in New York.

THE SECOND appearance at the Metropolitan Opera House of the two Russian dancers, Anna Pavlova and Mikhail Mordkin, was undoubtedly the feature of the performance which was given there last night for the benefit of the pension and endowment fund of that institution. The auditorium was packed for the occasion, and the total receipts were somewhere in the neighborhood of $15,000.

Very late in the evening before these two dancers had appeared in Delibes' ballet *Coppélia*. Last night they appeared alone without the assistance of the somewhat ragged *corps de ballet* of the Metropolitan Opera House in two divertissements, which were so entirely different from anything they had done in *Coppélia* that anyone who had seen their previous performance would have difficulty in recognizing them.

Such dancing has not been seen in New York in recent years, and last night's audience manifested its feeling as heartily as had that of Monday evening.

Early in the evening the curtains parted on a woodland scene which left a large open space on the stage. The orchestra played an adagio of Bleichmann's. First Mordkin darted onto the scene dressed as a savage. Pavlova followed him. The two danced together and then alone. Mordkin whirled for long seconds on one foot, with the other foot pointed at right angles from his body. He did another dance, in which he shot arrows from a huge bow behind his shoulder. The celerity, the grace, the rhythm of his terpsichorean feats were indescribable in their effect.

Pavlova twirled on her toes. With her left toe pointed out behind her, maintaining her body poised to form a straight line with it, she leaped backward step by step on her right foot. She swooped into the air like a bird and floated down. She never dropped. At times she seemed to defy the laws of gravitation. The divertissement ended with Pavlova, supported by Mordkin, flying through the air, circling his body around and around. The curtain fell. The applause was deafening. Again and again the two were called before the footlights.

Later in the evening the two danced again to music from a ballet of Glazunov's. This special divertissement was called *Autumn*. The music was gay and furious in its rhythm. The two in Greek draperies dashed about the stage, veiled in a background of floating gauze. The music became wilder and wilder, and wilder and wilder grew the pace of the two. The Bacchanalian finale, in which Pavlova was

finally swept to the earth, held the audience in tense silence for a moment after it was over, and then the applause broke out again. The curtain calls after this dance were innumerable.

TO SAY that history repeated itself yesterday afternoon at the Metropolitan Opera House, when Pavlova and Mordkin reappeared with their own company, to give for the first time here a program all by themselves, would be to express the case very mildly, indeed. It might almost be said that history was made on this occasion. It is doubtful if such dancing has ever been seen on the Metropolitan stage save when these two Russians were here last season, and it is certain that there never has been more enthusiasm let loose in the theater on a Saturday afternoon than there was yesterday.

The program included two complete ballets and several divertissements, and from 2:30 to 5:30, with intermissions now and then, Pavlova and Mordkin gave exhibitions of their highly finished and poetic art.

The afternoon began with a performance of Adolphe Adam's ballet *Giselle*, which has never been given before on

19

this stage and probably not often in New York, although it was seen here in 1842, one year after the original Paris production, which occurred at the Opéra, with Carlotta Grisi as the unhappy heroine.

The subject for the ballet was taken from Heinrich Heine's book about Germany. "There exists a tradition of nocturnal dancers, known in the Slavic countries as the *Wilis*. The *Wilis* are bethrothed girls who have died before their marriage. These poor creatures cannot remain tranquil in their tombs. In their hearts, which have stopped beating, in their dead feet, exists a love for dancing which they have not been able to satisfy during their lives. At midnight they rise and gather in troops, and unfortunate is the young man who encounters them. He is forced to dance with them until he falls dead.

"Garbed in their bridal robes, with crowns of orange blossoms on their heads and brilliant rings on their fingers, the *Wilis* dance in the moonlight like elves; their faces, although white as snow, are beautifully young. They smile with a joy so perfidious, they call you with so much seduction, their manner gives so many soft promises that these dead bacchantes are irresistible."

Théophile Gautier is said to have run across this passage one day and to have exclaimed involuntarily, "What a subject for a ballet!" However, he probably would have forgotten all about it if he had not encountered a composer at the Opéra that same evening. The result was that he and Saint-Georges collaborated on the book and Adam wrote the music. Coralli, the ballet master at the Opéra at that period, had enough to do with the book so that his name appears on the title page with the others.

This passage from Heine afterward attracted the eyes of other composers and librettists. The English composer, Loder, used the idea for his most successful opera, *The Night Dancers*, produced shortly after *Giselle,* and Puccini wrote his first opera, *Le Villi* on the same theme.

Carlotta Grisi danced the ballet and *Giselle* became the rage. Flowers, hats, gloves, dogs, and horses were named after her. The ballet was done almost immediately in England and America. But strangely enough, it disappeared from the repertoire of the opera until it was revived in 1863 with Mlle. Mouravieva, herself a Russian from Moscow. She was described by one critic of the day as having plenty of technique but "not an atom of poetry."

In Russia *Giselle* has always been popular, and Mrs. Newmarch says that it was Chaikovsky's ideal ballet when he composed his *Lac des Cygnes*. In Paris the past season has seen a revival of it, again by Russians.

The music is gently fragrant, a little faded here and there, but a pretty good score, and one of Adam's best. Cuts were made freely. In fact, almost one-half of the music had been taken out, and this was probably for the best, as far as the present-day audiences are concerned. There was one interpolation. In the first act a waltz from Glazunov's *Raymonda* was introduced, which was very much as if some conductor had performed *Also Sprach Zarathustra* somewhere in *Fra Diavolo*.

Mlle. Pavlova yesterday revivified this honeyfied and sentimental score of Adam's, full of the sad, gray splendor of the time of Louis Philippe. Grisi is said to have been gently melancholy in it, but Pavlova was probably more than that. Her poetic conception of the betrothed girl's madness when she finds her lover has deceived her, and her death, came very close to being tragic. It is almost impossible to describe the poetry of her dancing in the second act, where as one of the *Wilis*

she engages in the wildest sort of measures under the forest trees.

Mr. Mordkin had no dancing to do in this ballet, but in appearance and action he was superb. For some reason the program referred to the *Wilis* as "fairies," which can scarcely be regarded as an accurate translation.

The second part of the program consisted of divertissements beginning with a very pretty performance of Liszt's Second Rhapsody by Mme. Pajitzkaia, and the *corps de ballet*. After this Pavlova and Mordkin danced the Adagio of Bleichmann and the Chaikovsky Variation, in which they were often seen last year. After the bow-and-arrow dance, with which this divertissement concludes, it seemed as if Mr. Mordkin would never be able to leave the stage, the applause was so deafening and so long continued.

Some Russian dances followed to music from Glinka's *A Life for the Czar*, not by Chaikovsky, as the program stated, and this section of the program was completed with the Bacchanal from Glazunov's ballet, *The Seasons*, in which Pavlova and Mordkin swept the audience almost literally out of their chairs. To many this dance reaches the height of choreographic art.

Pavlova and Mordkin in *Bacchanale*. New York. Mishkin, 1910.

22

With Mordkin in *Bacchanale*. New York.
Mishkin, 1910.

Pavlova in *Bacchanale*. New York. Mishkin,
1910.

Pavlova and Mordkin in *The Legend of Ayziade*. New York. Mishkin, 1910.

Mordkin in his famous *Bow and Arrow Dance*. New York. Mishkin, 1910.

24

The ballet which concluded the program was called *The Legend of Azyiade*, and was doubtless suggested by a performance of Rimski-Korsakov's symphony *Scheherazade* as a ballet at the Paris Opéra last summer. However, Mordkin had arranged for this occasion an entirely different story, and the music was taken from many sources, although some of the themes from Rimski-Korsakov's symphony were retained. Among the dances introduced was one from Bourgault-Ducoudray's opera *Tamara*, distinctly Persian in character, and quite extraordinarily sensuous in its rhythm and tonal monotony. Several other composers, including Chaminade and Glazunov, were called upon to contribute.

Pavlova as the captive princess was as bewitching as possible, and Mordkin was so beautifully kinglike that many in the audience were heard to condemn the escape of the captive princess at the close as an unhappy ending.

The small group of dancers which accompanies Pavlova and Mordkin on this tour are most of them Russians and seems to indicate that in Russia as well as America Pavlova and Mordkin are unsurpassed. The *corps de ballet* appeared to special advantage in *The Legend of Azyiade*.

To Mr. Mordkin the highest praise is due for his work as a ballet master, for it was he who arranged the steps of all the dances and the program of the afternoon which contained just the correct amount of diversity.

Theodore Stier, the conductor of the Bechstein Hall concerts in London, made his first American appearance and gave an especially poetic reading of *Giselle*, and put the requisite amount of sensuousness into the music for the Arabian ballet. The orchestra's performance of the music to which Mr. Mordkin dances the bow-and-arrow dance would suggest that more rehearsals might benefit it, if it were not remembered that the Metropolitan Opera House orchestra last season never succeeded in playing it even respectably.

Pavlova at the age of twelve.

NOTES ON PAVLOVA PHOTOGRAPHS

by MARIANNE MOORE

"TO ENTER the School of the Imperial Ballet is to enter a convent whence frivolity is banned, and where merciless discipline reigns," Pavlova tells us in the autobiographic miniature entitled *Pages of My Life*. In keeping with that statement was her ability to regard genius as a trust, concerning which vanity would be impossible. "My successes," she said, are "due to my ceaseless labor and to the merits of my teachers." And yet, whereas the impression of security she gave could have been the result of an exacting discipline, for there have been virtuosi whose dancing was flawless, she was compelling because of spiritual force that did not need to be mystery, she so affectionately informed her technique with poetry.

Something of this we see in the photograph of her taken at the age of twelve—in the erectness of the head;

the absolutely horizontal brows indicating power of self-denial; the eyes dense with imagination and sombered by solicitude; the hair severely competent; the dress, dainty more than proud. "We were poor—very poor indeed"; ". . . my father having died two years after my birth," she says of childhood days with her mother in the country. "Bareheaded, and clad in an old cotton frock, I often would explore the woods close by the cottage. I enjoyed the mysterious aspect of the cloisterlike alleys under the fir trees" and "at times I wove myself a wreath of wild flowers and imagined myself to be the Beauty asleep in her enchanted castle."

Here are contrasts, romance unharmed by poverty and dreams that were ardor, recognizable in the very titles of parts danced in later years: the Butterfly, the Dragonfly, the Snowflake, Crystal Clear Spring, Fleur de

27

Lys's Friend, Giselle "the newborn fairy, daughter of the breeze." And as told by the memoir farther on, "In countries abroad, it was said there was 'something novel' in my dancing. Yet what I had done was merely to subordinate its physical elements to a psychological concept: over the matter-of-fact aspects of dancing—that is, dancing per se—I have attempted to throw a spiritual veil of poetry. . . ." So above all, it is affection for beauty that is unmistakable—which one might define as reverie which was reverence. Indeed in her "very first motion" wrote René Jean, "she seems about to embrace the whole world"; world being a term precise in more than the immediate sense, for in her dancing with persons, remoteness marked her every attitude. It is the uncontaminated innocence of her fervor that is really her portrait in the pose in which she is protectingly entwined with an actual swan —guarding and adoring what is almost a menace. Again the paradox of spirit contradictory with fact, in the autumn Bacchanal—her fingers resting as a leaf might have come to rest; and as the Dragonfly, she inclines the point of the left wing toward her head by the merest incurving touch of the fingers from below, as if there were on it silver dust or dew that must not be disturbed —while controlling the right wing by curving it over the wrist, with thumb and finger meeting upon the firmly held edge—though just within it. These truthful hands, the most sincere, the least greedy imaginable, are indeed "like priests, a sacerdotal gravity impressed upon their features"; yet—as noticed by Cyril Beaumont—they "were a little large for her arms, and the fingers inclined to be thick"; so the illusion of grace—though not accidental— must have been a concomitant of her subconscious fire; her expression, Mr. Beaumont continues, being as "changeable as the very face of nature; her body responding to the mood of a dance as a tuning fork vibrates to a blow": and in the fervently loyal reminiscences of her by Victor Dandré, her husband, we find that, losing patience with the lack of individuality in her dancers, she would say to them, "Why do you go about expressing nothing? Cry when you want to cry and laugh when you want to laugh."

Her feet, remarkable for the power of the ankle, their high arch, and "toes of steel," made her *pizzicati* on tiptoe, and steadily held pauses, possible; but not easy, as noted by Mr. Dandré, since her long main toe, by which the whole

Pavlova in *Christmas Night*. Hollywood, 1924.

weight of her body had to be borne, did not provide the squared support of the more level toes of the somewhat typically thickset virtuoso. Yet "when standing on one toe, she could change her entire balance," André Olivéroff says, "by moving the muscles of her instep. This may seem a small thing but it was one of the many that contributed to her dancing the perpetual slight novelty that made it impossible for an instant to tire of watching her."

"She is, I think, the most sincere woman it ever has been my good fortune to meet," was the feeling of Theodore Stier, musical director for her during sixteen years; "sincere with herself as with others"; and this doubly undeceived honesty was accompanied in her by logic. She did not admire Degas because he had delineated attitudes, not movement; and when inventing three social dances—the Pavlowana, the Gavotte Renaissance (not to be confused with the Gavotte Pavlova), and the Czarina Waltz—she took precaution that every step and pose should be within the ability of the average dancer. Her utter straightness of spirit was matched by an incapacity for subterfuge that is all but spectacular; as when in speaking of stage fright she admitted that each time before an

appearance she was subject to it, and "this emotion," she said, "instead of decreasing with time, becomes stronger and stronger. For I am increasingly conscious of . . . my responsibilities."

"Her feet are light as wings, her rhythm speaks of dreams," has been said by many in many ways; but if dreams are to transform us, there must be power behind them and in Pavlova the tirelessly unself-sparing dynamo, will power, by which she was to be incommoded and to incommode others, made itself felt when she was not more than eight. To celebrate Christmas, she was—for the first time—on her way to the Marinsky Theater with her mother, and inquiring what they were to see, was told, "You are going to enter fairyland." "When we left the theater," she says, "I was living in a dream. I kept thinking of the day when I should make my first appearance on the stage, in the part of the Sleeping Beauty." Begging to be allowed to enter the School of the Imperial Ballet, and refused by her mother, she then says, "It was only a few days later, wondering at my firmness of purpose, that she complied with my desire and took me to see the director of the school." Deferred by him until she was ten, since no child might be admitted earlier, she persevered after two years in persuading her mother to request admittance again, and was accepted. However tiring a journey might have been, "it was rare for her to go to her hotel in a town where she was to appear, before visiting the theater," says Mr. Stier, and in the draftiness of a darkened stage, she would practice while others rested. At rehearsal she was a "relentless taskmaster," we are told. Mr. Dandré says, "She was firm because she knew she was right." The word "firm" again; indeed ANNA PAVLOVA THE INCOMPARABLE PRIMA BALLERINA ASSOLUTA stamped in violet on the back of one of her St. Petersburg photographs is part of the likeness.

Will power has its less noble concomitant, willfulness, and although on occasion Pavlova could not be convinced that she was mistaken in giving aid to an impostor she pitied, or that she should desist from an over-impetuosity of which she might repent, she "did not know the meaning of the word 'cynicism.'" "Better thrice imposed on," she said, "than turn the empty away; . . . it is so easy to forgive people who must find it hard to forgive themselves." Willful and will-

powerful though she was, however, a modest deference of attitude was so natural to her that it marks her as all but one with the snowdrops and wild flowers she loved. Ever accurate, and wishing to make clear that the term ballerina is not used in speaking of a dancer who is merely one of the ballet, she unobtrusively uses the passive voice: "I left the Ballet School at the age of sixteen and shortly afterward was permitted to style myself Première Danseuse which is an official title. . . . Later I was granted the title Ballerina which but four other dancers of the present time have received." Here, again, a persuasion of contrasts: decisiveness with undogmatic precision; strength of foot with lightness of body; technical proficiency with poetic feeling; aloofness and simplicity in one who had chosen as her art that most exposed form of self-expression, dancing. It is said that "she proceeded intelligently, calmly, prudently" and that as she stood on tiptoe, the sole of her foot was "an absolute vertical—" a proof of "adequate training." Yet with the focused power, was an elfin quality or suddenness as incalculable as the fire in a prism—suggested by the darting descent to one knee, in the Dragonfly. "When she was excited about any-

31

thing," André Olivéroff says, "she had a way of clenching her hand and pressing it to her mouth, glancing sideways as though in search of a possible adventure—" May not this propensity to bewitchment explain the fact that she found irksome some of the portraits of her that others admire? And that she would try as she entered the theater, not to see the flaunted simulacrum of her displayed to attract patronage? Nothing is so striking as the disparity between her many likenesses; and nothing so eludes portraiture as ecstasy.

In dancing we have the rhythms of music made visible in space; also color and design; and if the result is to be more than acrobacy—power of dramatic expression. In each respect Pavlova was a creature apart: of slender form and aerial buoyancy—as noted above—with strength of foot, perfect technique which it was ever her study to "repair"; and interpretive power whereby she "acted the dancing and danced the acting."

Through its harmonized symmetries, style combines "the ability to disengage and co-ordinate elements"; and in her attitudes as in the timing of her steps, Pavlova possessed it. Balanced harmony, in her thinking and in her motions, was her very self. In the brief account of her life, having begun with the forest, she concludes with it: "The wind rustles through the branches of the fir trees in the forest opposite my veranda, the forest through which, as a child, I longed to rove. The stars shine in the evening gloom. I have come to the end of these few recollections."

So with pictorial symmetry. In the photograph taken at Ivy House, of her seated on the grass beside the chair of Maestro Cecchetti, her teacher of dancing, the descending line of the propped forearm, of her dress and other hand, of ankle and foot, continues to the grass with the naturalness of a streamer of seaweed—an inevitable and stately serpentine which imparts to the seated figure the ease of a standing one. Again, in the photograph in which she is seated on the wide shallow steps of a building in Italy—her hands on her sunshade which rests on her lap—the middle finger and little finger of each hand, higher than the finger between, adhere to classic formula but instinctively and with the resiliently spontaneous curve of the iris petal.

It seems to have been an idiosyncrasy of Pavlova's that one hand should copy rather than match the other, as in the Aimé Stevens portraits in which the hands, holding a string of jade and lifted as though to feel the rain, tend both in the same direction, from left to right (Pavlova's right), instead of diverging equilaterally with the oppositeness of horns. In Spring Flowers, the right foot turning left, is imitated by the left foot's half-moon curve to the left. Giselle—hands reaching forward, feet (tiptoe) in lyrelike verticals —is all of a piece. Everything moves forward together, like a fish leaping a weir; the tiny butterfly wings seen in silhouette, weighing the space above the level skirt that in soaring out, repeats the airy horizontal of the arms. And as with the swan curves of Giselle, so with the perfectly consolidated verticals in the Gavotte, the Dragonfly, and the Death of the Swan. Balance is master.

Spherical harmony of design would be lacking were it not for what does not show—the unremittingly perfected technique that made it possible. "The dancer," Pavlova said, "must practice her exercises every day." She must "feel so at ease so far as technique is concerned that when on the stage she need devote to it not a thought and may concentrate upon expression, upon the feelings which must give life to the dances she is performing." And we see how it could have been said of her, "it is as though some internal power impels the arabesque"; "even when engaged in extreme feats of virtuosity and bravura, she preserves spontaneity and ease." "I was essentially a lyric dancer," she says—a song that was a dance, if we are justified in taking that meaning from the Provençal ballada. She did not make the Italian mistake of introducing school exercises in her dancing, "never was interested in purposeless virtuosity," and would not, had she been able, have cared to outtire circus virtuosi who, suspended by teeth or wrist, revolve in a spinning blur for half an hour. "When she danced," Mr. Beaumont says, "the hands seemed delicate and the fingers tapering." "All her dancing was distinguished by absence of visible effort." "She turned pirouettes with an elegant ease, and though she rarely did more than two or three, she executed them with such a brio that they had the effect of half a dozen."

"The stage is like a magnifying glass. Everything tends toward exaggeration," and as in music, sensibility avoids misuse of the pedal, so with Pavlova, humor, esprit, a sense of style—and also a moral quality—made it impossible

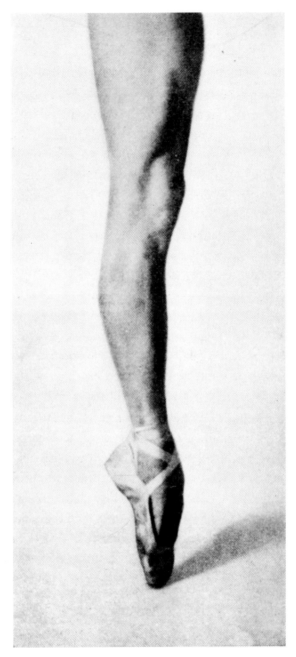

Pavlova's Point.

for her to show off, to be hard, to be dull; the same thing that in life made her self-controlled so that she was not a prison to what she prized; so that her punishment for what she deplored was apartness from it. "Her dancing," says Mr. Beaumont, quoting "a French writer," was "'la danse de toujours, dansée comme jamais'—the dance of everyday as it was never danced before"; and speaking of the 'Gavotte' danced to 'The Glowworm' music, by Paul Lincke, nothing could be more ordinary from the viewpoint of both choreography and music, yet she made it into a delicious miniature of the Merveilleuse period."

Although rhythm is the repetition of a sound or effect at regulated intervals, independence of rhythm is essential, and Pavlova never contented herself with literalities of technique; her inventions—the trill on tiptoe, the long pause on tiptoe, and the impulsive pirouette—being, indeed, a temperament's enlarging of accepted convention. "Her hands possess a life of their own," it was said, and one notes in the iris-petal fingers in the photograph with the sunshade the independence—that is to say the ultra-apartness—of the little finger from the fourth; the creative aptitude for fantasy, in the

double curve of the little finger; the originality of the slightly squared finger ends. These unfettered qualities seem to have something in common with a similar freedom in the dancing of Nijinsky, and with the pliant stateliness of Greta Garbo's comportment. One recalls, moreover, in connection with the independent fingers, Pavlova's choosing to appear at the Palace Theater in London and at the Hippodrome in New York. She indeed was, as someone remarked of her with unconscious skill, "a teaching."

A beautiful aspect of her independence was what Lincoln Kirstein has called the "openness" of her dancing, as when we see her in the Gavotte, advancing with the swirling grace of a flag and the decorum of an impalla deer. It recalls Mr. Olivéroff's saying, "I have sometimes felt that I would rather see her walk out upon the stage to take a curtain call than see her dance *Swan* or *Papillon*"; reanimating also her own statement, "Whatever a person does, or refrains from doing out of fear, is bad." Moreover, Mr. Beaumont says, "As the microphone amplifies the slightest sound, so her least movement held the attention of the audience," and we can understand how "she was never so successful in her ballets as in

35

Pavlova in *Don Quixote*. St. Petersburg, ca. 1908.

Pavlova in *Paquita*. St. Petersburg, ca. 1908.

Pavlova in *Divertissements*. St. Petersburg, 1906.

Pavlova in two divertissements. St.
Petersburg, 1906.

her soli and *pas de deux*"; how, "the ballet in being a composite work, . . . fell apart with Pavlova and her partner executing soli or *pas de deux;* the others coming on at intervals when it was necessary for the principals to rest."

Fairyland! It may be ecstasy but it is a land of pathos, and although Pavlova's parts were poetry, they were in most instances symbols of grief— Giselle, a wilis of the moonlight who must at dawn return underground from the world of light and love; La Péri, Servant of the Pure, who "realised that yon flower of life (the scarlet lotus) was not for her"; Crystal Clear Spring, the Ghost King's daughter, who warned her sisters not to open the door to the stranger and when they disobeyed and must die, chose not to be spared but die with them; Esmeralda, the forsaken gypsy who must dance at the festivities in honor of her betrayer; the Dying Rose, Valse Triste, the Death of the Swan.

Does imagination care to look upon a sculptured, a live, or any demonstrable fairy of the moonlight? What could constitute a greater threat to illusion than a seeming impersonation of the quiver of the dragonfly, or be less like a swan than two little wings arising unbiologically from the waist? It would seem that Pavlova was obliged to overcome her roles; and for the most part her costumes, for which she needed an Omar Khayyám, whose sense of structural continuity is poetry and whose novelty is to do without novelty. Mordkin's gladiatorlike torso might identify itself with his roles, whereas Pavlova was, theoretically, ever at a disadvantage. Is the motion picture of her Death of the Swan entirely becoming to her? Photographs of her dances, taken even at the good moment, fail, one feels, of the effect she had in life; and "those who never saw her dance may ask what she did that made her so wonderful. It is not so much what she did," Mr. Beaumont says, "as how she did it"; and one suspects that she so intently thought the illusion she wished to create, that it made her illusive—with hands and feet obeying imagination till there was no flaw to the eye. She had power, moreover, for a most unusual reason—she did not present as valuable the personality from which she could not escape. Of her Dying Swan, Mr. Beaumont says, "The emotion transferred was so overpowering that it seemed a mockery to applaud when the dance came to an end" and this impression given, of an aura of holiness resting upon her, is corroborated by

40

other observers; André Levinson's summary of that dance and its analogy with Giselle (the translation is here slightly altered), being a lament as well as a description: "Arms folded, on tiptoe, she dreamily and slowly circles the stage. By even, gliding motions of the hands, returning to the background whence she emerged, she seems to strive toward the horizon, as though a moment more and she will fly —exploring the confines of space with her soul. The tension gradually relaxes and she sinks to earth, arms waving faintly as in pain. Then faltering with irregular steps toward the edge of the stage—leg bones aquiver like the strings of a harp—by one swift forward-gliding motion of the right foot to earth, she sinks on the left knee—the aerial creature struggling against earthly bonds; and there, transfixed by pain, she dies."

"I imagine" . . . "I dreamed that I was a Ballerina and spent my whole life dancing, like a butterfly"; but her dance of the swan was a rite—arms resolutely folded, crusaderlike, in the sign of the cross—"the rhythms disintegrating" symbolically as in Giselle's dancing they disintegrated under madness, literally undoing her earthly joy. "Pavlova was simple, simple as a child is simple," André Olivéroff tells us,

"and yet there was a great tenderness about her, sadder than a child's and more peaceful." Why should one so innocent, so natural, so ardent, be sad? If "self-control is the essential condition of conveying emotion," and giving is giving up, we still cannot feel that renunciation had made Pavlova sad; may it have been that for lives that one loves, there are things that even love cannot do?

Of herself as she stood on the balcony of her hotel in Stockholm she says, "I bowed from time to time; and suddenly they began to sing. . . . I sought vainly for a way of expressing my gratitude. But even after I had thrown my roses and lilies and violets and lilacs to them they seemed loath to withdraw." And "following a brief season in Liége," Mr. Stier recalls Belgium's generosity: "When we went to settle with the various newspapers in which the performances had been advertised, to our astonishment, they refused to accept payment. 'Pavlova has done so much for the national appreciation of art,' they explained, 'that we cannot bring ourselves to accept money from her.'"

"How rare it is," she said to André Olivéroff—referring to certain members

Pavlova in *Giselle,* ca. 1910.

Pavlova in *The Swan,* ca. 1910.

Pavlova in *Coquetteries de Columbine*.

Pavlova in practice costume.

of her company—"to find an artist who combines passion with intellect, who dances always with a mind and body both trained, and with a heart that is on fire. Of the two, if I had to say, I would always choose the heart. But that alone is not enough. You must have both." In giving happiness, she truly "had created her crown of glory and placed it upon her brows." That which is able to change the heart proves itself.

ACKNOWLEDGMENTS

Publications consulted in preparing the foregoing commentary: Cyril W. Beaumont: *Anna Pavlova;* Cyril W. Beaumont, 75 Charing Cross Road, London, W.C. 2. 1932—Victor Dandré: *Anna Pavlova in Art and Life;* Cassell & Co. Ltd. 1932—New York Public Library "Iconography":—photographs; and as item 10, an advertisement folder describing the three social dances devised by Pavlova in 1914—the Pavlowana, the Gavotte Renaissance, and the Czarina Waltz—; announcing these dances with their music for the January, 1915, February, and March issues of *The Ladies Home Journal,* respectively.—André Olivéroff: *Flight of the Swan;* a Memory of Anna Pavlova as told to John Gill; E. P. Dutton, 1932—Theodore Stier: *With Pavlova Round the World;* Hurst and Blackett; no date.—*Pages of My Life* by Pavlova herself, translated by Sebastien Voirol—pages 115-130 in the V. Svetloff monograph—V. Svetloff (pseudonym) i.e. Valerian Yakovlevich: *Anna Pavlova;* with woodcuts by D. Galanis; published by Brunoff, 32 rue Louis-le-Grand, Paris. 1932—Carl Reissner-Verlag, Dresden, 1928: *Anna Pawlowa: Tanzende Füsse;* with Hänse Herrmann plates.—Quoted passages for which the source is not given, are to be found in the V. Svetloff monograph; also certain technical inferences from that work have been incorporated without stated acknowledgment. The illustrations are from the Dance and Theatre Collection and the Film Library of the Museum of Modern Art.

Pavlova in *Rondino*. New York. Mishkin, 1914.

Pavlova Portraits. Berlin, 1914.

46

Pavlova in rehearsal with her partner Volinine. Smallens at the piano with Clustine and Stier. New York, 1917.

Pavlova with Novikoff in *Valse Caprice*. London, 1911.

Pavlova with her pet swan Jack, at Ivy House, London, 1926.

Pavlova in *The Dragonfly*. New York, 1914.

Two poses in *The Dragonfly*. New York, 1914.

51

Pavlova and Volinine in *The Gavotte*. Time Photo, London, 1914.

With Novikoff in *Autumn Bacchanale*. London, 1911.

With Novikoff in *Snowflakes*. New York, 1921.

Pavlova in *The Swan*. New York, 1914.

Pavlova in *The Swan*. Hollywood, 1924.

Pavlova in *The Fading Rose*. Hollywood, 1924.

Pavlova in *Oriental Dance*. Hollywood, 1924.

Pavlova and Volinine in *The Gavotte*. New York. Mishkin, 1914.

APPENDICES

RECOLLECTIONS OF PAVLOVA

by MURIEL STUART

THERE have been numerous poems, books, and articles written about Pavlova the great artiste, dancer, and now legend. I would like to write of Pavlova, not as the artiste, dancer, or legend that is so well known, but as an influence, teacher, and mentor.

For me today, the qualities upon which she placed great value are the essence of all fine arts and never change. I am qualified to speak of these things in regard to Pavlova as I spent my formative years with her, being one of the eight children she selected to train. Many times she would have us remain after class and tell us of these qualities an artist must possess; namely, to observe people with whom we came in contact so as to be able to develop an awareness and a greater human understanding. In this way she pointed out that although she could train us to dance in class—to develop as a per-

son, and possibly an artiste, one had to have a cognizance and sensitivity to life in general.

To Pavlova technique alone was only a means to an end. She demanded that we be technically equipped but that we bring to our dancing something from within ourselves and thus make our stage personalities alive and vital. She deplored any pretensions or superficial attitude toward life or our work. Time and again she reminded us to approach both with reverence and humility.

As pupils our training was not limited to ballet technique alone. She arranged that we study many forms of the dance; Dalcroze, Spanish, Oriental, and Character. She took us personally to see many performances of great artistes, among them Mary Wigman and Isadora Duncan for whom she had a tremendous admiration. Her patience

61

and capacity for work were unbelievable. She would teach us for two hours
in the morning beginning at 10 o'clock.
We would assemble in the studio to
wait anxiously for her to come down
the stairs from her room which opened
onto a balcony. We knew by the color
of her dress whether she would be
happily disposed toward us or not. Our
favorite dress was a long and clinging
white one that she generally wore.
Then everything went well. But the
long black dress meant that she was

not feeling well and we all were sub-
dued—and very sad.

As a mentor she never failed to give
encouragement when it was needed.
Her great kindness and generous sym-
pathy toward sincere young people was
limitless. To many she was an inspiration and often after a performance she
would remain to give encouragement
and advice. Personally she enriched my
life so immeasurably that I shall always be grateful and devoted to her
cherished memory.

Pavlova in *Spanish Dance*. Chicago. Hutch-
inson, 1915.

Portrait. New York. Apeda, 1915.

Top left: Pavlova in her student days. St.
Petersburg, 1906. Top right: Pavlova in
The Sleeping Beauty. St. Petersburg, 1906.
Bottom: Pavlova in a *Pas Seul*. New York,
1921.

Pavlova in her dressing room at the Théâtre des Champs-Elysées. Paris, 1924.

CHRONOLOGY

1882 Born, St. Petersburg, January 31st.*

1892 Admitted to the Imperial Ballet School, St. Petersburg. First teachers: Paul Gerdt, Christian Johannsen, Nicholas Legat and Eugenia Sokolova.

1898 Leaves school.

1899 Makes debut at the Marinsky Theater in small part without ever having been a member of the *corps de ballet.*

1905 Begins study with Enrico Cecchetti.

1907 Tour to Riga, Helsingfors, Stockholm, and Copenhagen. First tour of a wholly trained company of Russian dancers. King Oscar of Sweden conferred Swedish Order of Merit on her.

1908 Tour to Leipzig, Prague, Vienna. Company included Adolph Bolm, Nicholas Legat, and Lubov Egorova.

1909 Appears with Nijinsky in *Le Pavillon d'Armide* for first Diaghilev Paris season at the Chatelet Theater. Dances *Le Cygne* at an invitation soirée for

* There seems to be considerable variance on the date of her birth. This is the date given by her husband Victor Dandré. Pavlova was an only child of poor parents, her father having died when she was two years old.

Edward VII and Queen Alexandra in London.

1910 American debut with Mordkin, Metropolitan Opera House, New York. Performs divertissements and ballet *Coppélia* with Metropolitan Company. Theodore Stier becomes musical director. First appearance with Mordkin at Palace Theater, London. Tour of English provinces.

1911 Returns, Palace Theater, London. Breaks with Mordkin and engages Laurent Novikoff as partner. Dances with Nijinsky in first Diaghilev London season. Principal roles in *Giselle, Cléopâtre, Pavillon d'Armide,* and *Les Sylphides.* Last appearance with Diaghilev company.

1912 Makes London permanent home. Purchases Ivy House, former residence of J. W. M. Turner, English painter.

1913 Tours Germany with new company recruited in England with extensive repertoire, including *Amarilla, Magic Flute, Fairy Doll,* and *Invitation to the Dance.* Spends several days with Jacques Dalcroze at Hellerau. Brief visit in Russia.

1914 Engages Alexander Volinine as partner. Tour of the United States and Canada. First of a series of grand tours.*

1915 Tours with Boston Opera Company. Same year accepts offer of Charles B. Dillingham to dance at the New York Hippodrome for $8,500 per week; two performances daily for six months. Personal prestige at highest peak. Presented divertissements with Volinine and her own version of ballet, *The Sleeping Beauty.*

1916 In Hollywood, played the leading role in the film, *The Dumb Girl of Portici,*† produced by Universal Pictures.

1917 Tour to Havana, dancing at the Teatro Nacional. Revolutionary days in

* Theodore Stier, her musical director, writing of these tours states that from 1910 to 1925 Pavlova and her company of dancers traveled over 300,000 miles, covering small towns and the largest cities all over the globe. They gave over 3,600 performances and over 2,000 rehearsals.

† Victor Dandré speaking of this film says: "There were several good moments in this film, but on the whole it was not a success. One thing was certain—Pavlova came out very well on the films . . . But she was only strengthened in the conviction that the film was not her sphere."

NOTE: This film is in the Film Archives of the Museum of Modern Art, New York City.

Cuba; attendance at performances very poor.

1918 Tour to South America and Mexico. Performed her Mexican National Dance on special Sunday matinées at Plaza de Toros for audiences of 25,000 persons. On tour through Mexico President Carranza ordered armed escort for her train.

1920 Establishes home for Orphans in Paris for White Russian refugee children. Funds solicited from all the countries where she had danced.

1922 Tour to Japan and the Far East.

1925 Tour through the continent. Spent several days with Mary Wigman at Dresden and expressed approval of Wigman's methods.

1927 Danced in London and the English provinces. Also tour of Germany and Italy.

1928 Last tour of South America. Engaged Pierre Vladimiroff, her last partner in Rio de Janeiro.

1929 Tour of Egypt, Java, India.

1930 Final tour of England. Last public appearance at Golders Green, December 13th. Danced *Giselle* with Vladimiroff as partner.

1931 Died at The Hague, Holland, January 23, 1931. Cremated and buried at Golders Green, London.

Pavlova with Enrico Cecchetti. St. Petersburg, ca.
1906.

Pavlova in *Bacchanale*. New York. Mishkin, 1910.

ANNA PAVLOVA BIBLIOGRAPHY

Anna Pavlowa's new flower ballet. *In* Theatre magazine, p. 42. New York, August, 1925.

Anna Pawlowa. Berlin, Verlag Bruno Cassirer, 1913. 43 pp. illus. (Contents: Anna Pawlowa, von Oscar Bie; Die Arten, von Paul Barchan; Der Tanz der Russen, von Max Osborn; Aus meinen Leben, von Anna Pawlowa.)

ARMITAGE, MERLE. Accent on America. New York, E. Weyhe, 1944. (Anna Pavlova, pp. 106-107.)

Autobiographia di una ballerina (Pavlova). *In* Comoedia. January, pp. 20-23; February, pp. 17-18. Milan, 1923.

BEAUMONT, CYRIL WILLIAM. Anna Pavlowa. London, C. W. Beaumont, 1932. 24 pp. illus.

BEAUMONT, CYRIL WILLIAM. Complete book of ballets. A guide to the principal ballets of the nineteenth and twentieth centuries. New York, G. P. Putnam's Sons, 1938. (Anna Pavlowa, pp. 639-641.)

BOLM, ADOLPH. Impressions of a partner before the world spotlight found Pavlowa. *In* Dance magazine, p. 14. New York, August, 1931.

CAFFIN, CAROLINE and CHARLES H. Dancing and dancers of today. The modern revival of dancing as an art. New York, Dodd, Mead and Company, 1912. (Anna Pavlova, Chap. 7.)

CHUJOY, ANATOLE. Ballet. New York, Robert Speller publishing corp., 1936. (Anna Pavlova, Chap. 7.)

CULL, A. TULLOCH. Poems to Pavlova; with eight illustrations of Madame Pavlova in her most famous dances. London, H. Jenkins, 1913. 62 pp. illus.

CULL, A. TULLOCH. To Anna Pavlova; roundel acrostic. *In* English Review, p. 9. London, August, 1912.

DANDRÉ, VICTOR. Anna Pavlowa. London, Toronto (etc.) Cassell and Company, Ltd. 1932. 409 pp. illus. ("Anna Pavlowa's repertoire," pp. 403-408.)

DANDRÉ, VICTOR. Anna Pavlowa. Ar autora atlauju tulkojis Valdemars Karklins. Riga, Gramatu draugs, 1935. 256 pp. illus. (Lettish translation.)

DEAKIN, IRVING. Ballet profile, by Irving Deakin. New York, Dodge Publishing Company, 1936. (Anna Palovna Pavlova, pp. 31-41.)

GENTHE, ARNOLD. The book of the dance. New York, Mitchell Kennerley, 1916. (Anna Pavlowa, Chap. 11.)

GRUNENBERG, ARTHUR. Anna Pawlowa. In Westermann's Monatshefte. Berlin, October, 1927. Pp. 165-172.

HASKELL, ARNOLD L. Balletomania: the story of an obsession. New York, Simon and Schuster, 1934. (Anna Pavlova, pp. 81-96.)

HASKELL, ARNOLD L. Ballet. A complete guide to appreciation; history, aesthetics, ballets, dancers. Harmondsworth, Middlesex, England, 1938. (Anna Pavlova, pp. 101-112.)

HOFFMAN, MALVINA. Pavlova in sculpture. In Vanity Fair, p. 38. New York, March, 1915.

D'HOUVILLE, GERARD. Herbier des songes; la Pavlova. In Revue des Deux Mondes, pp. 918-921. Paris, February, 1934.

HUSSEY, DYNELEY. Anna Pavlova. In Saturday Review, pp. 284-286. London, January, 1924.

HYDEN, WALFORD. Pavlova, by her former musical director. Boston, Little, Brown and Company, 1931. 258 pp. illus.

HYDEN, WALFORD. Pavlova, the genius of the dance. London, Constable & Co., Ltd., 1931. 199 pp. illus.

IVCHENKO, VALERIAN (Valerian Svetlov, pseud.). Anna Pavlova, translated from the Russian by A. Grey; woodcuts by D. Galamis. Paris, M. de Brunoff, 1922. 194 pp. illus.

IVCHENKO, VALERIAN. Anna Pavlova: some memories. In Dancing Times, pp. 685-689. London, March, 1931.

IVCHENKO, VALERIAN. Anna Pavlova, by Valerian Svetlov. London, British Continental press, 1931. 32 pp. illus.

IVCHENKO, VALERIAN. Anna Pavlova. Traduction française de W. Petroff. Bois gravé par D. Galamis. Paris, M. de Brunoff, 1922. 194 pp. illus.

IVCHENKO, VALERIAN. Memories of Pavlova and Diaghilev. In Dancing Times, pp. 531-536. London, September, 1933.

KARSAVINA, THAMAR. Obituary—Anna Pavlova. *In* Slavonic Review, pp. 725-726. London, March, 1931.

KEY, PIERRE. Pavlova of the twinkling toes. *In* Cosmopolitan, pp. 335-340. New York, February, 1910.

KINNEY, TROY. Anna Pavlova—a votive offering. *In* Dance magazine, pp. 18-19. New York, January, 1929.

LEGAT, NICOLAS. Anna Pavlova: some memories. *In* Dancing Times, pp. 683-684. London, March, 1931.

LEVINSON, ANDRÉ. Anna Pavlova. Paris, Grjébine et Vishgnak, 1928. 34 pp. 44 plates.

LEVINSON, ANDRÉ. Un cygne d'autrefois. *In* Les Annales Politiques et Littéraires, p. 473. Paris, May, 1928.

LEVINSON, ANDRÉ. La danse d'aujourd'hui. Études—notes—portraits. Paris, Editions, Duchartre et Van Buggenhoudt, 1929. (Anna Pavlova, pp. 115-140.)

LEVINSON, ANDRÉ. Les visages de la danse. Paris, Éditions, Bernard Grasset, 1933. (Anna Pavlova—Trépas du cygne, pp. 21-28.)

LEWALTER, ERNST. Unsterbliche Anna Pavlowa! Das Märchen ihres Lebens und ihrer Kunst. Dresden, Verlag Carl Reissner, 1938. 220 pp. illus.

LIEVEN, PRINCE PETER. The birth of Ballets-Russes; translated by L. Zarine. London, G. Allen, 1936. (Pavlova, Chap. 21.)

LONG, JUSTINE. When Pavlova was a little girl. *In* Bellman, pp. 570-571. Minneapolis, November, 1917.

MALVERN, GLADYS. Dancing star: the story of Anna Pavlova; illustrated by Susanne Suba. New York, Julian Messner, Inc., 1942. 280 pp. illus.

DE MEUSS, M. L. Star danced: Pavlova. *In* Cornhill magazine, pp. 549-551. London, May, 1932.

MEYERSTEIN, E. H. W. Elegy on the death of Mme. Anna Pavlowa. *In* New Statesman and Nation, p. 7. London, February, 1931.

MONROE, HARRIET. Pavlova dead: poem. *In* Poetry, a magazine of verse, p. 301. Chicago, March, 1931.

MOORE, LILLIAN. Artists of the dance. New York, Thomas Y. Crowell Company, 1938. (Anna Pavlova, pp. 210-215.)

MORGAN-POWELL, SAMUEL. Memories that live. Toronto, Macmillan Co., 1929. (Anna Pavlova, pp. 223-230.)

NOVIKOFF, LAURENT. Pavlova "Divine Revolutionist." *In* Dancing Times, pp. 20-24. London, October, 1925.

OLIVÉROFF, ANDRÉ. Flight of the swan; a memory of Anna Pavlova as told to John Gill. New York, E. P. Dutton & Co., Inc., 1932. 264 pp. illus.

OUKRAINSKY, SERGE. My two years with Anna Pavlova, by Serge Oukrainsky. Translated from the French manuscript by I. M. Los Angeles (etc.), Suttonhouse publishers, 1940. 196 pp. illus.

PAVLOWA, ANNA. Tanzende füsse; der Weg meines Lebens. Dresden, Verlag Carl Reissner, 1928. 124 pp. illus.

RABINOFF, MAX. Mlle. Anna Pavlowa. New York, Blanchford, 1914. 14 pp. illus. (Souvenir program.)

SAZONOVA, JULIE. Anna Pavlova. *In* Revue Musicale, pp. 303-313. Paris, April, 1931.

STIER, THEODORE. With Pavlova round the world. London, Hurst & Blackett, Ltd., 1927. 288 pp. illus.

Tänze von Anna Pavlowa im Bilde. Dem Gedächtnis der Künstlerin dargebracht. Dresden, Verlag Carl Reissner, 1931. 32 plates.

TURNER, W. J. Popular Pavlova. *In* New Statesman, pp. 644-645. London, September, 1924.

VESELO, ANDREW. The immortal swan. *In* Sight and Sound (note on Pavlova film). London, Spring, 1946.

Top: Pavlova with her pet terrier. Paris, D'ora, 1914. Bottom left: With Novikoff in *Amarilla*. New York, 1914. Bottom right: Pavlova in *Coquetterie de Columbine*. New York, 1924.

Pavlova with Stowitts in *Syrian Dance*. Buenos Aires, 1917.

Pavlova and Novikoff in *The Egyptian Mummy*. London, 1921.

74

Pavlova and Stowitts in *Syrian Dance*. Buenos Aires, 1917.

Pavlova and Novikoff in *The Egyptian Mummy*. London, 1921.

75

Pavlova with Pianowski in *Gavotte*. London, 1913.

Pavlova with Novikoff in *Valse Caprice*. Paris, 1913.

Pavlova and a cameraman in Hollywood. 1916.

Anna Pavlova in the film, *The Dumb Girl of Portici.*
Hollywood, 1916.

ACKNOWLEDGMENTS

Anna Pavlova's *Pages of My Life* is republished with the kind permission of Michel de Brunoff, Paris. The translation by Sebastien Voirol is from the Russian edition of Valerian Svetlov's excellent monograph, "Anna Pavlova," Paris, Michel de Brunoff, 1922.

Carl Van Vechten's "Pavlova at the Metropolitan" is republished from *Dance Index,* Vol. 1, September-November, 1942, with the gracious permission of the author and by courtesy of *The New York Times* where these reviews first appeared on the following dates: March 1, 2, 18, and October 16, 1910.

Marianne Moore's article is also a reprint from *Dance Index,* Vol. 3, March, 1944, and Muriel Stuart, teacher at the School of American Ballet, has generously given us her "Recollections of Pavlova" for this book.

Most of the photographs were generously lent by the Department of Theater Arts and the Film Library of the Museum of Modern Art. The photograph of Pavlova with her husband is from the collection of Eudekia Mironowa, Pavlova's costumer for twenty years.

Isadora
Duncan

Isadora Duncan. Photo by Arnold Genthe. New York, 1916.

PREFACE

THE YEAR 1947 marks the twentieth anniversary of the death of a distinguished American dancer, Isadora Duncan. An embodiment of the American spirit, fearless, honest and direct, with a burning love of freedom, she passionately believed in dancing as the great art. Indeed her first awareness of herself was as a dancer—a dancer who wanted to move freely and embrace the whole of humanity. She was in a sense our first American dancer since those in this country who preceded her—Mary Ann Lee, Augusta Maywood, George Washington Smith and others—were concerned primarily with the formal European tradition of theatrical dancing. It was Isadora who first brought to Europe and then to her own country, a new attitude—her own vision of America Dancing.

Isadora's particular genius as a person as well as an artist has probably evoked more contemporary interest than any other theatrical personality of her time. The legend that she has left is still subject to special scrutiny and the particular school that followed her (although she was personally against the notion of schools and traditions) based on her "technique" is today probably not at all a reflection of her principles and style, since these were qualities inherent in Isadora, the person and artist, and hence were nontransferable. However, in the vast body of contemporary modern dance her notions on dancing are widely manifested and it is apparent that her indirect influence on Fokine and subsequently the Russian Ballet have made possible certain innovations which persist today.

In this series of essays and commentaries on Isadora there is further evidence of her unique personality and greatness. The notes on her early concerts in New York are as fresh and vital after thirty years as if they had been written yesterday, while the comments on Isadora and basic dance contribute more substantially to our understanding of her than anything which has appeared since her autobiography. The interest in her as a subject for artists is indicated in the range of paintings, drawings, and sketches which are reproduced in this book. These together with the various photographs illuminate in some measure the quality of Isadora the dancer and of her boundless personality.

ACKNOWLEDGMENTS

THE MATERIAL in this book is made up largely from issues of the periodical, *Dance Index*, and I am grateful to Mr. John Martin, Mr. Carl Van Vechten, and Mr. Allan Ross Macdougall who have graciously given me their permission for the use of this unique material. I am also indebted to *The New York Times* for permission to reprint Mr. Van Vechten's pieces on Isadora which appeared in *The New York Times* on the dates noted in the article. I acknowledge with thanks the permission of Alfred A. Knopf to reprint *The New Isadora*, which first appeared in Carl Van Vechten's book *The Merry-Go-Round*, 1918. Captain Edward Steichen has permitted me to publish his excellent photograph of Isadora at the Parthenon, and Mr. George Chaffee has been kind enough to loan me the study of Isadora by Gordon Craig. Mr. George Amberg of the Department of Theatre Arts, the Museum of Modern Art, has made available to me the excellent material in his department and Mr. Edwin Denby located two rare photographs of Isadora taken in Munich. It is through their courtesies that this book is being published and to them I extend my warmest thanks.

CONTENTS

Isadora
Duncan

Isadora Duncan and Basic Dance

AN OUTLINE FOR DANCERS

BY JOHN MARTIN

IT IS a curious thing that in all the reams that have been written about Isadora Duncan there is so little with any specific bearing upon her art. There are tributes aplenty, eulogies and poems, word-pictures of the personal states she inspired in her spectators, and romantics of all kinds frequently bordering on the fulsome, but virtually nothing is to be found that examines objectively what she did and sets it forth in orderly terms with reference to its permanent values and formulable principles. To all intents she might have been a transient phenomenon floating across time in her scarves to no more purpose than a meteor. Yet actually she is greater now than she was while her comparatively short and stormy career was going on, and will become greater still as the inertia of mass thinking continues to dissolve with the passing of time and the import of her accomplishment becomes clearer.

She herself saw but was, of course, never reconciled to the unavoidability of this time lapse. Of her countrymen she asked rhetorically from overseas when they would quit neglecting her, see the purpose of her work and make it possible for her to carry on; and she answered her own question with the prophecy that fifty years after her death they would build a monument to her. Less than fifteen of these years have yet gone by but the prophecy is already beginning to be fulfilled. The monument that is building, however, is not the conventional tribute in stone which she foresaw, but a body of living dance freely acknowledging her as its source. It is still struggling as she struggled against indifference, to some extent, but what is more of a handicap, it is still working largely through intuition as she was forced to work, in spite of the fact that her very efforts have made this no longer a necessity.

Isadora has left scattered through her brief writings a fully rounded theory of the dance which is generally not suspected, and it is time to add to the already crowded bookshelf devoted to her one volume which undertakes to look beyond personality and to order and elucidate this material. Such a task adequately performed would result in probably the greatest textbook of the dance ever written. It is not to be accomplished, however, by him who writes as he runs. It demands insight into an altogether intuitive mind pitting itself against respected inertias and entrenched bigotries; it further demands courage to read between the lines in order to see the things that Isadora herself did not know she saw, and to penetrate the surface limitations of a period as well as of an individual who, though she belongs among the great ones of the earth, had her prejudices and predilections, conscious and unconscious. It is a job for an intensely practical mind, able not only to extract the universal theory from a highly personal art, but, once that is done, to reparticularize it in terms of contemporary practice.

This would entail discoveries and adaptations that would surprise and shock Isadora herself, if she could learn of them, for great concepts frequently grow beyond the grasp of those who have earliest enunciated them. Take, for example, the way we talk today of democracy not only as a political and social philosophy, but also as an economic one, and compare it with the ideas of so notable a pioneering democrat as Thomas Jefferson, who was not even in favor of universal male suffrage. Yet it is the same concept, acted upon by the changing demands of the times and by its own growth from within. Our textbook compiler must be able to establish as definite a nucleus of Isadora's fundamental concept and keep it clear through its various changes of aspect in her own and others' application of it. Especially must he be wary of the roseate mist that surrounded it in the days of its birth. Isadora "freed" the dance. From what? For what? From corsets and shoes, Minkus and Delibes, pointes and port de bras? For Chopin wa

Wagner operas and Chaikovsky symphonies in bare feet and Greek tunics? If she

only a creator of styles in movement, music and dress, she was of minor importance and only indifferently successful, for all these innovations are already obsolete. In that case, let us proceed with the erection of the dolorous marble monument of prophecy, a sentimental monstrosity dictated by idolatry and memorialism and destined to make coming generations look on the legend of Isadora with something not far removed from contempt.

Instinctively one knows in the face of what has happened in the dance itself of recent years that such a theory is false, but rationally there is no specific body of facts to build upon. Only our temerarious scribe can supply the means for doing justice to an artist of epochal importance and what is more to the point, for protecting her magnificent heritage. No mere scholiast will serve, adding a timorous footnote here and an apologetic paraphrase there. It must be someone who will vigorously dispel the clouds, reduce what he finds beneath them to the simplest fundamental terms, and boldly fill what gaps he uncovers.

II

Let us see, in broad outline, what his textbook must include.

In the first place, Isadora was not concerned with establishing a new school of dancing, called the Duncan Dance, or what you will. She was militantly opposed to schools, systems, and professionalism in general. What she was primarily concerned with can only be called basic dance—not a trade or a profession or even an art to begin with, but a biological function. She was not seeking to invent or devise anything, but only to discover the roots of that impulse toward movement as a response to every experience, which she felt in herself and which she was convinced was a universal endowment. Without benefit of formal psychology, she knew as no other dancer on record had known that spontaneous movement of the body is the first reaction of all men to sensory or emotional stimuli. Though civilization tends to dull and to inhibit this tendency, it is still the fundamental reaction of men to the universe about them.

Isadora Duncan. New York City. Schloss, 1898.

A revival of the conscious use of this faculty would mean deepening and broadening the whole range of life. If the individual becomes aware of the world in which he lives through its direct effect upon his nerves and muscles, nature's fundamental perceptive mechanism, he has won his freedom from the arbitrary thou-shalts and shalt-nots which established social cults and creeds put upon him the moment he is old enough to be dominated. Only when he has developed the power to touch life at first hand does he begin to be aware of his inherent selfhood, and until he has become thus aware he cannot develop his true bent or resist the forces that would conventionalize him into a mass product.

This was and is a colossal concept, not only affecting the dance but virtually adding another dimension to life. It plays havoc with categories, upsets tradition, destroys rote and official revelation. Yet its theory has been eloquently enunciated both in words and in its own stuff of responsive movement by Isadora, it has been practiced by a generation of other dancers through a kind of subconscious transfer and advanced by them far beyond the rational grasp of its laws, and it is now quite possible for our textbook to present it in terms of a logical and workable technical procedure. All that is required, besides the qualities of insight, courage, and practicality already enumerated, is a thorough knowledge of anatomy, psychology, esthetics and education!

Isadora, however, without any scientific equipment whatever, has indicated all the true directions and many of the exact roads to be traveled. She has related how, once she had become convinced through her own experience that movement arose from a central inner source which she called the soul, she sought to find where in the body this source was located and how it was to be stirred to action. The word "soul" is likely to frighten us today, but if it is allowed to do so we will miss the whole point of Isadora's basic dance. For her it meant simply that correlative of the mind which produced, instead of intellectual concepts, quite irrational expressions of feeling. It was no more confined to a physical organ than the mind is confined to the brain, but she felt that it must have some correlative "habitation" in the body. For hours she stood before the mirror in a concentration that suggests the Orient, seeking this bodily center, and the conclusion of her quest was amazingly analytical. Through watching, apparently quite objectively, her emotional and motor impulses and relating them to each other, she discovered to her complete satisfaction that the solar plexus was the bodily habitation of the soul and the center in which inner impulse was translated into movement. If we are to take her literally at her word and accept the fact that by these solitary experiments she was able actually to isolate internal nervous experience in this way, it is one of the most astounding accomplishments on record. But even if she began with a considerable basis of theory, her discovery remains remarkable for its soundness in relating emotion to visceral action and visceral action to outward movement. She had, however crudely and in whatever inaccurate and unscientific terminology, discovered the soul to be what less imaginative men have called the autonomic system.

On this revolutionary principle she based all her practice and her teaching, and our textbook must do likewise until a greater researcher arises to supersede it. But a principle without a technique to make it operative is merely an abstraction, and here Isadora arrived at less tangible results. Her efforts, however, are a guide as well as a check upon more specific methods that may (and must) be devised by others.

How to start the motor in the soul, as she once phrased the impulsion to move? Her own chief means was music—Wagner, Beethoven, all the great romanticists of the nineteenth century—music which stirred the emotions; but she knew that this was not the solution and said so. Nor was this the only means she employed. She surrounded her young pupils with paintings and sculpture to form their standards of action visually, and she turned them to the processes of nature for the same end. Presumably besides listening to music "with the soul" they were to be guided subconsciously by the ideal of living beauty which was held before their eyes.

But most important of all her approaches to the subject were the experiments she made not with stimulation by other arts but directly with personal emotion. She has described her search for certain key movements which should arise out of elemental emotional experiences such as fear and love, and from which a whole series of developing movement should flow as of its own volition. These experiments were important for several reasons, but to the present topic they are of especial significance. She has told us nothing at all about her mode of procedure in these experiments, but it can easily be supplied from the context, and in it lies the answer to the problem. Here we find her deliberately invoking specific emotional states without music or any other external aid, and the only possible means that lay within herself was memory. In order to discover a "first movement" of fear from which a sequence of related and developing movements should proceed in natural order, a state resembling fear itself must be re-created to stimulate the impulses of suitable movement. This could only be done by recalling previous experiences of fear and allowing these memories freely to induce their own bodily and emotional states.

Isadora made use of certain actual phrases of movement discovered by these experiments, but she did not carry the method itself through to its full development, and missed accordingly the basic technical process of her art. A colleague, however, did carry it through in another art and for slightly different ends. This was Constantin

London. Dover Street Studios, 1910.

Stanislavsky of the Moscow Art Theater who demanded from his actors the same kind of emotional truth, arising from the same kind of inner impulsion, that Isadora demanded from herself and all dancers. His use of affective memory as the root of the actor's technique was more deliberate than Isadora's and consciously shaped into a clear-cut, teachable method for training actors.

To reconcile the differences between an actor's technique and a dancer's need is the first major task of our textbook. The actor, at least as Stanislavsky saw him, works in terms of naturalism, while the dancer, in Isadora's sense of the word, deals in great abstractions of human experience; but it is the same truth that underlies both their arts, for they are in essence only one art in different guises. Already, however, considerable experimentation has been done in adapting the principles of Stanislavsky to the problems of the dancer, and the textbook, therefore, need not be delayed for any prolonged research along uncharted ways. It is possible immediately to present an orderly method for starting Isadora's motor of the soul, avoiding all the pitfalls that threatened her and using ultimately the very principles that she found for herself without knowing she had done so. It need remain no longer a vague and inspirational process.

III

But this is the beginning rather than the end of the problem. Even though it is possible to produce technically by the conscious use of affective processes motor reactions that are honest and true, it does not necessarily follow that dance movement has been produced. Dance movement is not a mere succession of motions, however inspired, but exists in terms of sustained dynamic tone, just as song is not a mere succession of sounds but exists in terms of sustained vocal tone.

It was music that supplied the necessary transforming element for Isadora. If it served first of all to lower the threshold of motor activation for her, it also provided a continuity of impulse. As long as its emotional qualities had power to stir her, she was provided with an impetus to evolve a continuum of movement, so to speak, of genuinely responsive character. She had learned to make herself so sensitive to this kind of impul-

Isadora Duncan. Munich. Elvira, 1902. (Courtesy Edwin Denby)

sion that she could sustain movement with unfaltering emotional truth through entire symphonies. It was only under this form of stimulation, she declared, that she was able to rediscover "the natural cadences of human movements," but obviously this did not satisfy her as a basic method, for instead of giving herself up to it indulgently and considering the matter closed, she set about searching for tangible, controllable technical means. Significantly enough, in the two important phases of this search—the location of the "central crater of motor power" and the evocation of "first movements"—she eschewed the use of music altogether.

It is these experiments in the production of "first movements" that must here concern us once more. In them she was aiming not merely at the production without external stimulation of creative motor responses, but at the production of motor responses each of which should result in a sequence of movement unfolding along the line of its specific

9

La Marseillaise. New York. Arnold Genthe, 1916.

emotional origin. Such a sequence implies inherent continuity of tone as well as progression in a consistent direction. It is a parallel in its own medium of the phrase in music and was probably being sought as such by Isadora. Certainly the example of music was not absent from her mind, for though she worked in silence she declared that these movements "seemed to create themselves from the rhythm of some invisible music." A sequence of movement flowing as if of its own volition from a single emotional impulse is actually a motor phrase, the lowest common denominator of dance movement and the basic unit of composition. It is the transformation of the simple feeling-acting technique, which produces individual expressive motions known as gestures, into the broader and more intensive stuff which we call movement and of which art is made.

Isadora apparently made no formal adaptation whatever of these extraordinary experiments to her teaching methods. There is an intuitive awareness of the character of the motor phrase, perhaps, in her insistence that the exercises of her young pupils always have an entity of their own and never lapse into isolated movements or mere muscular exertion. What she may have done in this field when she led her classes into improvisations it is impossible to tell, but certainly she left no definite instructions for teaching the individual discovery of "first movements" and the development of the motor phrase.

Again our pedagogue must turn to Stanislavsky for general guidance if not for specific instructions. The method of improvisation is undoubtedly indicated here; first, for the gradual strengthening of the ability to sustain emotion, and second, for the recognition of the natural tendency of emotion thus sustained to feed upon itself, resulting, almost literally of its own volition, in invention and perception that the individual is unaware of possessing. Stanislavsky's practices along these lines are helpful but too literal on the one hand and too diffuse on the other, for the dancer must concentrate his responses into the motor field exclusively and must lift them completely out of the category of merely expressive gesture. This is a by no means impossible transition, but it increases immeasurably the dangers, which already inhere in Stanislavsky's method, of auto-hypnosis and virtual nervous debauchery. It is extremely perilous ground on which our pedagogue treads here, and if he turns back fearing his responsibility, he need not consider himself cowardly. Many dancers have turned back here, for the work enters the rather despised field of pure self-expression, at best, and from there may easily wander off into pathological regions. If he is the true pedagogue that he must be to undertake such a textbook, however, he will know how to erect the necessary controls which the artist-dancer, who is not necessarily a pedagogue at all, will not know how to erect. Actual experimentation has already been done in the dance field which eliminates these hazards and the chief task in so far as the textbook is concerned is to reduce the experimentation to orderly principles and teachable practices. A delicate job, if you will, but a perfectly feasible one, and without it there is no earthly way of insuring the translation of inner emotional impulsion directly into the stuff of the dance.

IV

Thus far the problem has been altogether a subcutaneous one, so to speak; but the instrument of the dance is the outward body, and its adjustment to the demands made upon it is quite as important as the demands themselves. The greatest potential singer in the world armed with the most magnificent songs can do nothing unless he has an adequate voice and complete control of it, and the dancer is in the same situation. He not only needs to know how to play his instrument, but he must also build it out of himself and keep it tuned at all times. It is not enough that the body which is his instrument is a healthy enough body to take him through his daily living without limitation or disturbance; the body of the dancer is no more the half-conscious vehicle that carries him about from home to business, fumbling with hats and coats, papers and carfare, than the singer's voice is the sound-making apparatus with which he orders his coffee and chats about the weather. The dancer's body is a totally sentient organism capable of encompassing movements far more extended in range and dynamism, speed, and elasticity, than those encountered in routine living. It makes no difference at all that in his dancing he is dealing with the impulses and experiences of nature, projecting only the passions of men, and not attempting acrobatic feats, contortions, or any movements that violate nature; he is nevertheless not dealing in naturalistic gestures and so-called life movements, for he is presenting an idealization, an interpretation, a concentration of life experience, which because it is less diffuse than actuality must be correspondingly more intense.

How, then, to prepare the body for this larger-than-life function? Isadora was convinced that some form of gymnastic training was necessary before dance training as such could begin, but she is not specific about what it should consist of. There are certain things, however, that she knew it should not consist of, and these help to clear the ground. First, it must not be mere muscle development. The dancer is not a professional strong man whose business it is to flex his biceps, lift weights, and put shot; neither his individual musculature nor his skills are ends in themselves and it is worse

Isadora and her husband, the Russian poet, Essenin. New York, 1922.

than useless to develop them as such. Worse because the body is a wonderfully efficient organism which, for the conservation of its energy, makes everything habitual as quickly as possible. In order to avoid sending every incoming impression through the whole taxing process of emotional awareness and conscious examination, it establishes short cuts at the first opportunity by which familiar stimuli can be shunted off immediately to familiar reactions practically automatically. Thus the exercises which through repetition enlarge muscles soon become associated with no other function, and result in movement that is emotionally barren and the very reverse of expressive. The dancer's habit of moving must be made such that movement is never an end in itself but always the outward result of an inward awareness.

It follows, then, that no series of set movements, whatever their virtues for muscle development, can be established as a training technique. It does not matter whether they are devised according to an impersonal, scientific plan, or are merely an adaptation of some individual artist's personal inspiration crystallized into a vocabulary. The dancer must be trained neither to make somebody else's movements nor to resort to mechanically contrived routines, but quite to the contrary every ounce of his energy must be directed to the task of moving in his own highly personal and essentially unique manner. Obviously, the exercises by which he builds his bodily technique must consist accordingly of movements drawn out of himself as responses to emotional stimuli, but calculated at the same time to extend his physical capacity along all the required gymnastic lines.

Isadora met this problem in a way that is certainly too simple for the wider field of today, but that is nevertheless indicative of her intentions and perhaps even of a line of practical development. Her exercises (and there is no indication that the gymnastics that she advocated as pre-dance training were given to her young pupils through any other channel) consisted of movement processes common to everybody in the round of ordinary experience—walking, running, skipping, leaping, and the like. In making use of these materials she was assuredly putting nothing arbitrary or external upon the pupils, but was taking advantage of natural and, indeed, inevitable motor patterns of their own as a basis for operation. Though they were far too habitual even in young children to be considered as inherently creative movement, she actually reoriented them so that they were in large measure creatively produced. Whether or not this was possible with any but young children, or even invariably with them, is open to question, but it was definitely accomplished in many cases. To see such elementary movements as these performed in this way is to realize how little elaboration and extravagance of movement are necessary to command attention, to achieve a transfer of emotional experience and to provide genuine artistic satisfaction, when there is a complete unison of inward prompting and outward manifestation.

Because Isadora's dance was simple in its gymnastic demands, she was undoubtedly able to develop all the needed strength, elasticity and endurance under cover of these natural movements. But for increased requirements along these lines, her method (or at least this aspect of it) remains substantially sound with only a corresponding increase in dimensions. Actually the different types of movement of which the body is capable are remarkably few; tension and relaxation, flexion and extension, rotation, torsion and transfer of weight come pretty close to covering the entire range in broad terms. If our inspired pedagogue will only devise themes for improvisation with emotional demands designed explicitly to result in each of these necessary elements of movement and to bring into play in turn and in conjunction the various parts of the body, he can succeed in his more intensive medium as Isadora succeeded in her simple one. If he is really qualified to prepare this exemplary textbook, he can evolve a thorough and practicable method for the vigorous technical training of the dancer's body without resorting to a single superimposed routine or a solitary example of formal gymnastics. He will not, perhaps, produce acrobats thus, but he will produce dancers, provided always that he has talent to work with.

V

Another element in this pre-dance gymnastic training has to do with guarding the individuality of every dancer's style of movement. Isadora's use of natural movement for training purposes at least recognized the existence of the problem, but did not attempt to solve it, at its source. It is all very well to call walking, running and skipping natural, but they are natural to the race rather than to the individual. Every individual will walk and run differently according to his bodily formations and those less tangible aspects of his personality which we call his temperament; what then is the natural way to walk? Is there some ideal racial norm that must be discovered and imitated? If so, is this natural to the individual who, left to his own devices, will behave otherwise? If not, is whatever way the individual happens to walk natural to him even if it is perhaps caused by some muscular or nervous abnormality? Is deformity or eccentricity the same thing as individuality? If so, might it not be the better part of wisdom just to forget all about preserving individuality and begin superimposing harmonious routines that will obscure it?

If we are to encourage the individual to move according to his particular endowments, it is incumbent upon us at the same time not to encourage him to emphasize his weaknesses to his ultimate destruction. First, obviously, we must help him to establish his norm. This will involve consideration of basic body mechanics, the correction of postural misalignments and the removal of the psychic disturbances of which they are frequently the result. Here, again, our erudite pedagogue will have to call in an expert, for he has found the juncture of the dance with therapy of a closely related type. Much of the work will be done by methods curiously akin to that which lies at the center of Isadora's theory, for in making these postural and mechanical adjustments in the body, the most advanced practice makes use of mental imagery to produce reactions in deep muscles that are not under voluntary control. However, our textbook, being thorough and consistent, will inevitably demand not only theoretical quotations but also personal tuition from a "body mechanician"—a Mabel Elsworth Todd, for example, or a Lulu Sweigard or a Margaret Paulding, who stem from her teaching directly or indirectly —both for the establishment of the individual norm in the first place and for frequent periodic checks to make sure that it is being maintained. Until some such practice is instituted, talking about natural movement and the preservation of individuality is just so much loose and romantic verbiage. And that is exactly the stuff that our whole project is designed to destroy.

VI

Here, perhaps, would end the first volume of the textbook. By means strictly in accord with Isadora's theory but employing the best contemporary technical developments, it has produced a dancer. There is much more, indeed, to be treated of from the same source and in the same manner before the subject is finished. The dancer, once produced, must learn to compose his dances, to choose his music, to design his costumes, and the basis of his procedure is admirably set forth in principle in Isadora's essays and autobiography. For all the Pre-Raphaelite sense of beauty that is commonly attributed to her, she has argued eloquently for what is sometimes called ugliness, and her method of evolving form out of content is worthy of the deepest study; her restoration of the body from exile is still not understood or practiced as it should be; and even in her attitude to music, the least amenable of her theories, there are pregnant hints about modern music and the future in general.

Our newly made dancer must have an insight into the rather profound esthetics of his great preceptor in order to allow her to lead him into paths which she herself never traveled. He will discover, for one thing, that her dance was lyric because all art is lyric in the beginning. The artist first gives expression to his personal emotions, even though he may couch them in heroic and impersonal terms. (Isadora "never once danced a solo," but "tried always to be the Chorus.") Next he materializes a protagonist, a concentrated figure who dances with the chorus; and finally an antagonist emerges as well—and the theater is born. The lyric base has not been destroyed but augmented, and the contemporary trend of the dance toward the theater can find orderly principles for its procedure in Isadora's lyric precedent.

All that, however, is for Volume Two.

Isadora in *La Primavera*. Paris, ca. 1900.

Duncan Concerts in New York

BY CARL VAN VECHTEN

November 10, 1909

Miss Isadora Duncan, who has evolved a style of choreographic art which corresponds in a measure at least—according to a comparison with the figures on ancient vases—with the dances of the ancient Greeks, made her reappearance in New York last evening at the Metropolitan Opera House, assisted by Walter Damrosch and the New York Symphony Orchestra.

The program stated that Miss Duncan would dance to the ballets and choruses of *Gluck's Iphigénie en Aulide*. Most of her dances were accomplished to such aid, but at least one of them, a Chorus of Priestesses, was taken from *Iphigénie en Tauride*, and its original purpose and signification were greatly distorted by the dancer. It is a number which was never designed for dancing, and to anyone who has heard it in its proper place in the opera it must seem more or less of a sacrilege to have it put to such purpose.

There can be no possible objection, however, to Miss Duncan's appropriating the ballet numbers from the Gluck operas for her particular purpose. It is a well-known fact that Gluck composed many of his ballets because they were demanded by the audiences of his time rather than by the exigencies of his operas. It is also quite as true that the list of them includes much that is best of the Gluck music.

They are particularly fitted in their nobility and lack of sensuousness to accompany the moods and poses which Miss Duncan portrays in her dances. She is at her best in dances which depict life and gaiety and motion. In this she is always sure of communicating her meaning to an audience. The Bacchanale which ended the formal program exhibited her finest talents. The play of the arms in the moderato and allegro in which the Maidens of Chalkis play at ball and knuckle bones by the seashore was also one of the effective bits.

The dances last night were in nowise different from those in which Miss Duncan has appeared in past seasons in this country and Europe, and her draperies were the same beautiful Greek arrangements. Repetitions of several of the dances were demanded by the large audience, and at the end of the program Miss Duncan added several extra numbers, concluding with *The Beautiful Blue Danube* waltz.

November 17, 1909

Miss Isadora Duncan again appeared at the Metropolitan Opera House yesterday afternoon and danced for the first time this season to Beethoven's A major symphony, which was played by the New York Symphony Orchestra, with Walter Damrosch conducting. It is quite within the province of the recorder of musical affairs to protest against this perverted use of the Seventh Symphony, a purpose which Beethoven certainly never had in mind when he wrote it. Because Wagner dubbed it the "apotheosis of the dance" is not sufficient reason why it should be danced to.

However, if one takes it for granted that Miss Duncan has a right to perform her dances to whatever music she chooses, there is no doubt of the high effect she achieves. Seldom has she been more poetical, more vivid in her expression of joy, more plastic in her poses, more rhythmical in her effects than she was yesterday. Wagner's title for the symphony might very properly be applied to Miss Duncan. As usual, she was most effective in the dances which require decisive movement. One of the wildest of her dances she closed with arms outstretched and head thrown back almost out of sight until she resembled the headless Nike of Samothrace.

The orchestra played Chaikovsky's *Marche Slave*, a pantomime from Mozart's ballet music to *Les Petits Riens*, and a Beethoven *Polonaise* for the second part of the program and then Miss Duncan danced five Chopin numbers. The audience was large and enthusiastic.

February 16, 1911

Miss Isadora Duncan, the American girl who is directly responsible for a train of barefoot dancers who have spread themselves, like a craze, over two continents in the last five years, has returned to America, and yesterday she gave a new exhibition of her dancing, with the assistance of Walter Damrosch and the Symphony Society, at Carnegie Hall. Before the doors opened there were no seats to be had, and the long line of carriages which drew nigh the portals, as the hour set for the dancing to begin approached, indicated that Miss Duncan not only was the first of the barefoot dancers, but also the last. She not only has established her vogue, but she has also maintained it.

It has long been the custom for Miss Duncan to dance to music which originally belonged either to the opera house or the concert room. In years gone by she has lifted her feet to Chopin measures; to dances from the Gluck operas; and even to Beethoven's Seventh Symphony. This last was considered by many as a desecrating escapade, but many others paid money to see her do it, and Miss Duncan achieved some of her greatest popular success with the symphony which Wagner called the "apotheosis of the dance." Doubtless many people thereby became acquainted with a work of Beethoven which they never would have heard otherwise.

Yesterday Miss Duncan forsook the masters who have given her most of her material for dancing until now. She had arranged, in fact, an entirely new program, through which to display her art. It was made up of excerpts from the Wagner music dramas and Bach's *Suite in D*.

If Bach did not intend that his music should be danced to, at least several of the numbers in this suite bear the names of dances, so Miss Duncan cannot be taken too much to task for employing them for her purposes.

The stage setting was what it usually is at a Duncan séance. Green curtains depended from the heights of the stage and fell in folds at the back and sides leaving a semi-circular floor in the center on which dim rose-colored lights flitted here, contrasting with shadows there. When Mr. Damrosch came to the conductor's desk and raised his baton, all the lights in the auditorium were extinguished. The orchestra played the prelude to the suite and then Miss Duncan appeared.

Autograph photo for Mary Fanton Roberts, ca. 1911. (Courtesy M. F. Roberts)

She wore, as she always does, some drapery of diaphanous material. She stood for a moment in the shadow at the back of the stage while the orchestra began the *Air*, the celebrated slow movement in the suite, which violinists play on the G string. Miss Duncan waved her arms and posed during this movement but did not do much of what is conventionally called dancing.

In the two Gavottes and the Gigue which followed, however, the dancer was seen at her best. She flitted about the stage in her early Greek way and gave vivid imitations of what one may see on the spherical bodies of Greek vases. The Bourée from the suite the orchestra played alone and the first part of the program closed with the Polacca from the first *Brandenburg Concerto*, also undanced.

There was a brief intermission before the Wagner excerpts were played. Then the house was darkened and the *Lohengrin* Prelude was performed. After this Miss Duncan gave her interpretation of the Flower Maidens' music from *Parsifal*.

This time she appeared in white gauze, beautifully draped. Her hair was caught up with flowers of pinkish hue. She evidently danced with an imaginary "Guileless Fool" standing in the center of the stage. To him she appealed with all her gestures and all her postures. It was an interesting attempt to give the spirit of the scene in the Klingsor's garden. What it meant to those who have never heard Wagner's music drama this writer cannot profess to know.

The next number announced on the program was the Prelude and *Liebestod* from *Tristan und Isolde*. Instead, however, of rapping for attention from his orchestra, Mr. Damrosch asked the audience for attention, turned about, and made a little speech.

The purport of his remarks was to the effect that it had originally been intended that Miss Duncan dance only music which had been arranged by Wagner in his music dramas for that purpose.

"It had been my intention," said Mr. Damrosch, "simply to play this music from *Tristan*. Yesterday, however, Miss Duncan modestly asked me if I would go through the *Liebestod* with her. She has, as is well known, a desire to unite dancing to music in a perfect whole, as an art which existed in the time of the early Greeks. Whatever she does now, of course, must be largely experimental. However, the results which she

23

has already achieved with the *Liebestod* are so interesting that I think it only fair to set them before the public. As there are probably a great many people here to whom the idea of giving pantomimic expression to the *Liebestod* would be horrifying, I am putting it last on the program, so that those who do not wish to see it may leave."

There was applause and then Miss Duncan gave her impressions of the Paris version of the Bacchanale from *Tannhäuser*, which were very pretty but hardly as bacchanalian as might have been expected. After the orchestra had played the Prelude to *Die Meistersinger* she danced the Dance of the Apprentices from that music drama. It may be stated that Miss Duncan did her best dancing of the afternoon to this number and it was repeated.

As for the *Liebestod*, the anticipation of it evidently was not too horrible for anyone to bear. People did not leave their seats, except possibly the usual few who are obliged to catch trains. Miss Duncan's conception of the music did not seem to suggest a pantomimic Isolde, nor was it exactly dancing. In other words, she puzzled those who knew the music drama, and did not interest those who did not. Therefore one may ask, Why?

February 21, 1911

It was to the operas of Gluck that Miss Isadora Duncan went for her first inspiration when she began her revivals of the Greek dance, and yesterday afternoon in Carnegie Hall she returned to Gluck. Her previous attempt to dance to the music from the lyric dramas of Richard Wagner had not resulted in complete success, but her spectators yesterday were pleased to see that Miss Duncan was herself again.

The first half of the program consisted of copious excerpts from *Orfeo*, played in chronological order, and embracing the chief incidents of the book, with the exception of the scene in which Eurydice persuades Orpheus to turn and gaze upon her face. The Symphony Society of New York, Walter Damrosch conducting, played the music; a small chorus, seated among the orchestra, sang several of the choruses, and Mme. Florence Mulford sang several of Orpheus's airs.

In the first act, in a long robe of flowing gray, Miss Duncan represented one of the companions of Orpheus. Her poses and movements were intended to suggest the deepest grief. It was in the first scene of the second act, that of the scene in Hades, which was given in its entirety, that Miss Duncan, portraying one of the Furies, first aroused the enthusiasm of the audience. She indicated the gradual wavering of the Furies from the tremendous "No" in the beginning to the end when the Furies allow Orpheus to pass on to the Elysian Fields. The Dance of the Furies, with which this scene concludes, was a remarkable exhibition of dancing, evidence of high imagination.

It had originally been intended that several of the choruses and Orpheus's air from the scene of the Elysian Fields should be included in the program scheme, but evidently it was found necessary to omit these. Only the ballet airs were presented from this scene, including the famous air with flute obbligato, which was exquisitely played by Mr. Barrère.

Miss Duncan, as a Happy Spirit, was as much at home as she had been previously as a Fury. From here on a long excision was made in the score until the finale was reached; even the famous chaconne was omitted. In the final scene, in which the chorus again appeared, Miss Duncan indicated the triumph of Love.

The excerpts were beautifully played by Mr. Damrosch and his orchestra. It is worthy of note that the seldom heard overture, a usually omitted ballet air, and the finale, which is replaced at the Metropolitan Opera House by a finale from another opera of Gluck, were restored. As has been stated, much else was omitted.

After an intermission Miss Duncan danced to some music by Schubert, and the orchestra played Dvořák's *In the Spinning Room*.

At the Parthenon, 1920. Writing in her autobiography *My Life*, Isadora reports: "The painter Edward Steichen who was one of our party took many lovely pictures in the Acropolis and in the theatre of Dionysius which faintly foreshadowed the splendid vision I longed to create in Greece."

The New Isadora

BY CARL VAN VECHTEN

I HAVE a fine memory of a chance description flung off by someone at a dinner in Paris; a picture of the youthful Isadora Duncan in her studio in New York developing her ideals through sheer will and preserving the contour of her feet by wearing carpet slippers. The latter detail stuck in my memory. It may or may not be true, but it could have been, *should* have been true. The incipient dancer keeping her feet pure for her coming marriage with her art is a subject for philosophic dissertation or for poetry. There are many poets who would have seized on this idea for an ode or even a sonnet, had it occurred to them. Oscar Wilde would have liked this excuse for a poem . . . even Robert Browning, who would have woven many moral strophes from this text. . . . It would have furnished Mr. George Moore with material for another story of the volume called *Celibates*. Walter Pater might have dived into some very beautiful, but very conscious, prose with this theme as a spring-board. Huysmans would have found this suggestion sufficient inspiration for a romance the length of *Clarissa Harlowe*. You will remember that the author of *En Route* meditated writing a novel about a man who left his house to go to his office. Perceiving that his shoes have not been polished, he stops at a boot-black's and during the operation he reviews his affairs. The problem was to make 300 pages of this! . . . Lombroso would have added the detail to his long catalogue in *The Man of Genius* as another proof of the insanity of artists. Georges Feydeau would have found therein enough matter for a three-act farce and d'Annunzio for a poetic drama which he might have dedicated to "Isadora of the beautiful feet."

Sermons might be preached from the text and many painters would touch the subject with reverence. Manet might have painted Isadora with one of the carpet slippers half depending from a bare, rosy-white foot.

There are many fables concerning the beginning of Isadora's career. One has it that the original dance in bare feet was an accident. . . . Isadora was laving her feet in an upper chamber when her hostess begged her to dance for her other guests. Just as she was she descended and met with such approval that thenceforth her feet remained bare. This is a pretty tale, but it has not the fine ring of truth of the story of the carpet slippers. There had been barefoot dancers before Isadora; there had been, I venture to say, distinct "Greek dancers." Isadora's contribution to her art is spiritual; it is her feeling for the idea of the dance which isolates her from her contemporaries. Many have overlooked this essential fact in attempting to account for her obvious importance. Her imitators (and has any other interpretative artist ever had so many?) have purloined her costumes, her gestures, her steps; they have put the music of Beethoven and Schubert to new uses as she had done before them; they have unbound their hair and freed their feet; but the essence of her art, the spirit, they have left in her keeping; they could not well do otherwise.

Inspired perhaps by Greek phrases, by the superb collection of Greek vases in the old Pinakothek in Munich, Isadora cast the knowledge she had gleaned of the dancer's training from her. At least she forced it to be subservient to her new wishes. She flung aside her memory of the *entrechat* and the *pirouette*, the studied technique of the ballet; but in so doing she unveiled her own soul. She called her art the renaissance of the Greek ideal but there was something modern about it, pagan though it might be in quality. Always it was pure and sexless . . . always abstract emotion has guided her interpretations.

In the beginning she danced to the piano music of Chopin and Schubert. Eleven years ago I saw her in Munich in a program of Schubert impromptus and Chopin preludes and mazurkas. A year or two later she was dancing in Paris to the accompaniment of the Colonne Orchestra, a good deal of the music of Gluck's *Orfeo* and the very lovely dances from *Iphigénie en Aulide*. In these she remained faithful to her original

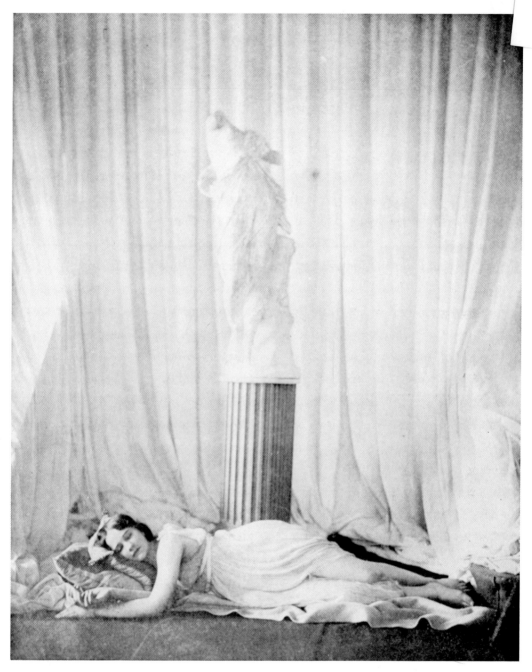

The Isadora Duncan Studio at Nice, ca. 1926.

ideal, the beauty of abstract movement, the rhythm of exquisite gesture. This was not sense echoing sound but rather a very delightful confusion of her own mood with that of the music.

So a new grace, a new freedom were added to the dance; in her later representations she has added a third quality, strength. Too, her immediate interpretations often suggest concrete images. . . . A passionate patriotism for one of her adopted countries is at the root of her fiery miming of the *Marseillaise*, a patriotism apparently as deep-rooted, certainly as inflaming, as that which inspired Rachel in her recitation of this hymn during the Paris revolution of 1848. In times of civil or international conflagration the dancer, the actress often play important roles in world politics. Malvina Cavalazzi, the Italian ballerina who appeared at the Academy of Music during the Eighties and who married Charles Mapleson, son of the impresario, once told me of a part she had played in the making of United Italy. During the Austrian invasion the Italian flag was *verboten*. One night, however, during a representation of opera in a town the name of which I have forgotten, Mme. Cavalazzi wore a costume of green and white, while her male companion wore red, so that in the *pas de deux* which concluded the ballet they formed automatically a semblance of the Italian banner. The audience was raised to a hysterical pitch of enthusiasm and rushed from the theater in a violent mood, which resulted in an immediate encounter with the Austrians and their eventual expulsion from the city.

Isadora's pantomimic interpretation of the *Marseillaise*, given in New York before the United States had entered the World War, aroused as vehement and excited an expression of enthusiasm as it would be possible for an artist to awaken in our theater today. The audience stood up and scarcely restrained their impatience to cheer. At the previous performances in Paris, I am told, the effect approached the incredible. . . . In a robe the color of blood she stands enfolded; she sees the enemy advance; she feels the enemy as it grasps her by the throat; she kisses her flag; she tastes blood; she is all but crushed under the weight of the attack; and then she rises, triumphant, with the terrible cry, *Aux armes, citoyens!* Part of her effect is gained by gesture, part by the massing of her body, but the greater part by facial expression. In the anguished appeal she does not make a sound, beyond that made by the orchestra, but the hideous din of a hundred raucous voices seems to ring in our ears. We see Félicien Rops's "Vengeance" come to life; we see the *sans-culottes* following the carts of the aristocrats on the way to execution . . . and finally we see the superb calm, the majestic flowing strength of the Victory of Samothrace. . . . At times, legs, arms, a leg or an arm, the throat, or the exposed breast assume an importance above that of the rest of the mass, suggesting the unfinished sculpture of Michael Angelo, an aposiopesis which, of course, served as Rodin's inspiration.

In the *Marche Slave* of Chaikovsky Isadora symbolizes her conception of the Russian moujik rising from slavery to freedom. With her hands bound behind her back, groping, stumbling, head bowed, knees bent, she struggles forward, clad only in a short red garment that barely covers her thighs. With furtive glances of extreme despair she peers above and ahead. When the strains of *God Save the Czar* are first heard in the orchestra she falls to her knees and you see the peasant shuddering under the blows of the knout. The picture is a tragic one, cumulative in its horrific details. Finally comes the moment of release and here Isadora makes one of her great effects. She does not spread her arms apart with a wide gesture. She brings them forward slowly and we observe with horror that they have practically forgotten how to move at all. They are crushed, these hands, crushed and bleeding after their long serfdom; they are not hands at all but claws, broken, twisted piteous claws! The expression of frightened, almost uncomprehending, joy with which Isadora concludes the march is another stroke of her vivid imaginative genius.

In her third number inspired by the Great War, the *Marche Lorraine* of Louis Ganne, in which is incorporated the celebrated *Chanson Lorraine*, Isadora with her pupils, symbolizes the gaiety of the martial spirit. It is the spirit of the cavalry riding gallantly with banners waving in the wind; the infantry marching to an inspired tune. There is nothing of the horror of war or revolution in this picture . . . only the brilliancy and dash of war . . . the power and the glory!

Of late years Isadora has danced (in the conventional meaning of the word) less and less. Since her performance at Carnegie Hall several years ago of the *Liebestod* from

Tristan, which Walter Damrosch hailed as an extremely interesting experiment, she has attempted to express something more than the joy of melody and rhythm. Indeed on at least three occasions she has performed a Requiem at the Metropolitan Opera House. . . . If the new art at its best is not dancing, neither is it wholly allied to the art of pantomime. It would seem, indeed, that Isadora is attempting to express something of the spirit of sculpture, perhaps what Vachel Lindsay describes as "moving sculpture." Her medium, of necessity, is still rhythmic gesture, but its development seems almost dreamlike. More than the dance this new art partakes of the fluid and unending quality of music. Like any other new art it is not to be understood at first and I confess in the beginning it said nothing to me, but eventually I began to take pleasure in watching it. Now Isadora's poetic and imaginative interpretation of the symphonic interlude from César Franck's *Rédemption* is full of beauty and meaning to me and during the whole course of its performance the interpreter scarcely rises from her knees. The neck, the throat, the shoulders, the head and arms are her means of expression. I thought of Barbey d'Aurevilly's, *"Elle avait l'air de monter vers Dieu les mains toutes pleines de bonnes œuvres."*

Isadora's teaching has had its results but her influence has been wider in other directions. Fokine thanks her for the new Russian Ballet. She did indeed free the Russians from the conventions of the classic ballet and but for her it is doubtful if we should have seen *Scheherazade* and *Cléopâtre. Daphnis et Chloë, Narcisse* and *l'Après-midi d'un Faune* bear her direct stamp. This then, aside from her own appearances, has been her great work. Of her celebrated school of dancing I cannot speak with so much enthusiasm. The defect in her method of teaching is her insistence (consciously or unconsciously) on herself as a model. The seven remaining girls of her school dance delightfully. They are, in addition, young and beautiful, but they are miniature Isadoras. They add nothing to her style; they make the same gestures; they take the same steps; they have almost, if not quite, acquired a semblance of her spirit. They vibrate with intention; they have force, but constantly they suggest just what they are . . . imitations. When they dance alone they often make a very charming but scarcely overpowering effect. When they dance with Isadora they are but a moving row of shadow shapes of Isadora that come and go. Her own presence suffices to make the effect they all make together. . . . I have been told that when Isadora watches her girls dance she often weeps, for then and then only she can behold herself. One of the griefs of an actor or a dancer is that he can never see himself. This oversight of nature Isadora has to some extent overcome.

Those who like to see pretty dancing, pretty girls, pretty things in general will not find much pleasure in contemplating the art of Isadora. She is not pretty; her dancing is not pretty. She has been cast in nobler mold and it is her pleasure to climb higher mountains. Her gesture is titanic; her mood generally one of imperious grandeur. She has grown larger with the years—and by this I mean something more than the physical interpretation of the word, for she is indeed heroic in build. But this is the secret of her power and force. There is no suggestion of flabbiness about her and so she can impart to us the soul of the struggling moujik, the spirit of a nation, the figure on the prow of a Greek bark. . . . And when she interprets the *Marseillaise* she seems indeed to feel the mighty moment.

July 14, 1917

Water color and pencil drawing. Auguste Rodin. Paris, ca. 1906.

Isadora Duncan and the Artists

BY ALLAN ROSS MACDOUGALL

AT VARIOUS TIMES during her later years, Isadora Duncan was heard to say, when questioned about the genesis of her dance: "I sprang full-fledged from the head of Zeus!" We who knew and loved her never quite dared challenge the dogmatic statement, although we knew that her art, like many such manifestations of genius, was a rare plant of slow and continual growth. We knew, and of course Isadora also knew, that the final, full flowering of her dance bore slight semblance of relation to the first wrinkled seed planted within her, who knows how or when.

Through the years the seed was watered by many rains and its first frail sprout warmed by many suns. The growth of the plant was nurtured and encouraged by many outside influences; occasionally it was pruned by self-criticism. Whatever dancing the young Californian did in her childhood days in San Francisco and her early travels across the continent to New York, certainly bore no relation to that exhibited at her tremendous final performance in Paris in 1927, the 49th year of her life. The innocuous little pieces mimed with Delsartean gestures to music by Ethelbert Nevin and the lesser Romantic composers, were childish, fumbling, clay-modeled figurines compared to the heroic, the monumental works such as César Franck's *Rédemption*, or the *Tannhäuser Overture* and *Bacchanale*, which were only part of that last performance at the Mogador Theater.

In her early days Isadora's dance was always referred to as *Greek*. This, doubtless, because she adopted flowing Greek draperies and performed her dance with feet and

Isadora Duncan. Pastel drawing by Fritz von Kaulbach. Munich, 1902. (Used as a cover for the magazine *Jugend*, 1904.)

arms bare; she also confessed quite frankly that she studied Hellenic sculpture and vase paintings.

"During my youth," she once wrote to the editor of the French daily, *Progrès d'Athènes*, "I spent long hours of admiring enthusiasm before the Parthenon and its friezes, the frescoes, the Greek vases, the Tanagras, not with the idea of copying them or their attitudes, or the divine expression of these masterpieces, but really, after studying them at length, to try and get right to the depths of their primordial being and to attempt to discover the 'secret' of their ecstasy through spiritual exploration of the symbolic ideas of their gestures. From their mystery came my dance—not Greek, not Antique, but in reality the expression of my soul moved to harmony by Beauty."

From photographs it can be seen that in the '90's Isadora neither dressed *à la Grec* nor skipped about with unshod feet. Certain studio photographs taken in 1898 in New York, show the 20-year-old dancer wearing ballet slippers and a dress fashioned of lace. According to all accounts it was not until she had reached Europe and had met and been influenced by the English Philhellenes and the artists of Paris, that her dance became "free." The tentative shoot from the wrinkled seed began to open out, drinking in with avidity the warmth of the new climate of art and appreciation to which it had been transplanted.

If in her later years Isadora gave much to painters and sculptors so that she became, without any doubt, the most portrayed woman in the world, it is certain that in these early years at the turn of the century, she also received much inspiration and unspoken direction from artists with whom she associated. And together with the marvelous Greek collections of the British Museum and the Musée du Louvre, William Blake also contributed his share of inspiration and direction. I used to own, until some bibliophilic pilferer purloined it from Djuna Barnes to whom I had lent it, the dancer's copy of the Gilchrist *Life of Blake*. The copious marginal notes in the handwritings of Isadora and of Gordon Craig attested to a diligent study, not only of the text but also of the illustrations.

Isadora's own story of her brief career in England where she gave what, for want of a better phrase, is called "drawing-room entertainments," in the London houses of the gentry, and danced the First Fairy and other minor choreographic roles with the traveling Shakespearean company of the late Frank Benson, has been told in her autobiography. The English experience was merely a repetition, with cultural differences, of her life and art in New York, even down to her theatrical essays in dancing.

The turning point of Isadora's career as a dancer was undoubtedly her first visit in the year 1900 to Paris, the supreme capital of European art and culture. Then it was that she spent long hours and many days studying the Greek vases in the Louvre. With her brother Raymond—a gaunt young man who had not yet adopted his quasi-Greek get-up of hand-woven chiton and chlamys and hand-tooled sandals—the young visitor made the rounds of all the museums and monuments of the City of Light. "There was

Isadora Duncan's Berliner Tanzschule

Berlin, 1904. Caricature from the magazine *Jugend*. "In this period we shall finish with Mr. Beethoven. In the next we shall begin on Mr. Aeschylus." "Leave that alone Frau Duncan, and teach us Mr. Richsdorfer instead." (Richsdorfer was the name of a popular ragtime dance, taken from a Berlin suburb.)

not a monument," she later said, "before which we did not stand in adoration, our young American souls uplifted before this culture which we had striven so hard to find."

It was in that fateful year of 1900, at the exciting Exposition Universelle, that Isadora felt the tremendous impact of the double-barreled revelation of the marble and bronze of Auguste Rodin and the great tragic dancing of the Japanese artist Sada Yacco. These two experiences left indelible impressions on her sensitive mind. And with the youthful Californian intensity with which she was pursuing culture, Isadora and her English companion, Charles Halle, visited the Rodin Pavilion innumerable times, and night after night sat through the performances of "the wondrous art" of the famous Oriental dancer.

Through a nephew of Halle, Isadora was introduced into the world of art and artists after having been presented to Madame de St. Marceau at whose salon she danced one evening. Then followed a series of recitals given in various fashionable salons frequented by members of the French aristocracy and the reigning figures of the musical, artistic, and literary worlds—André Messager, André Beaunier, Jean Lorrain, Henri Bataille, the Comtesse de Noailles, Madeleine Lemaire, the Prince and Princesse Edmond de Polignac, and Eugène Carrière, to mention only a few of the better known names.

With the latter great artist, the American dancer became quite intimate. She was introduced into his humble and affectionate family circle. He painted her portrait in his monochromatic, vaporous style, a wholly different Isadora and completely divorced from the dancing figure portrayed so many times by other artists. Later in her more affluent days she bought two of Carrière's canvases which she always treasured and which she finally parted with under the stress of extreme poverty. So delighted was the paternal Carrière with her dancing that he prepared notes for a brief *causerie* which he delivered before one of her performances in a Paris salon, sometime in 1901.

"Isadora, wishing to express emotions," he wrote, "discovered in Greek art her finest models. Full of admiration for the lovely figures of the bas-reliefs, she adopted them as her inspiration. Yet, endowed with the instinct of discovery, she returned to Nature from whence came all these gestures, and thinking to imitate and give rebirth to Greek

Crayon drawing by Leon Bakst. Russia, 1908.

Portrait in oils by Eugène Carrière. Paris, ca. 1909.

Pen drawings of Isadora by Jean-Paul Lafitte. Paris, ca. 1909.

dancing, she found her own expression. She thinks of the Greeks and obeys but herself; she offers us her own joy and her own grief. In demonstrating to us her fine feelings so beautifully, she evokes ours: as before Greek statues revivified a moment for us, we are young again with her and a new hope triumphs within us. And when she expresses her resignation to the inevitable we also resign ourselves.

"Isadora Duncan's dance is no longer an entertaining diversion; it is a personal manifestation as well as a work of art, livelier and more fecund as an incentive to works which we ourselves are destined to do."

From this fruitful period in Paris dates not only the dancer's acquaintance with Rodin's work but also with the artist himself. Having admired almost daily his statues shown in the Rodin Pavilion at the Exposition, she finally made her way to the master's studio. This first meeting ripened into a very real mutual friendship and admiration for each other's art. Like the gentle and humble Carrière, the genial sculptor had a decided influence upon the young dancer. Later she was to rent one of the studios near him in the disused convent building, rue de l'Université, where Rodin created some of his noblest works.

In the year 1903, to celebrate Rodin's promotion to the rank of Commander of the Legion of Honor, a group of his pupils and intimate friends—among them Besnard, the distinguished painter, the sculptor Bourdelle, Octave Mirbeau, Fritz von Thaulow, and some others less well-known then—arranged an *al fresco* party at Vélizy, near Chaville, on the outskirts of Paris. Impromptu speeches were made and von Thaulow played his violin. Then, according to Frederick Lawton, who in 1907 wrote the first biography of the French master:

"Miss Isidora [sic] Duncan, an American lady, known in Paris for her rhythmic interpretations of Beethoven's music, rose and danced on the greensward, resuscitating as far as might be the terpsichorean art of old."

Here the stodgy Victorian biographer is less enthusiastic than his subject. For Rodin publicly expressed his whole-hearted appreciation of the art of the new dancer. He also made rapid sketches of her as she danced at various times. "It can be said of Isadora," he wrote, "that she has attained sculpture and emotion effortlessly. She has borrowed from Nature that force which cannot be called Talent but which is Genius.

"Miss Duncan has properly unified Life and the Dance. She is natural on the stage where people rarely are so. She makes her dance sensitive to line and is as simple as the Antiquity synonymous with Beauty. Suppleness, emotion, these high qualities which are the soul of the dance, are her complete and sovereign art."

The studies Rodin made of the dancer, like his equally well-known series of the Cambodian dancers, were rapid, calligraphic sketches, retouched with a thin, watercolor wash. They are interesting, of course, and highly personal, but lack the precision of the younger Bourdelle's innumerable sketches of the dancer, or even those done by a sculptor of lesser fame, José Clara.

This young Catalan was one of an enthusiastic band of artists who attended en masse the first public performances given by Isadora in Paris. I recall his telling me that for the first performance, fearing the hall might not be filled, Raymond and Isadora ap-

43

peared at the Ecole des Beaux-Arts and distributed to the astonished students, *billets de faveur*—or Annie Oakleys as Broadway jargon has it.

At these early recitals the young art students were the most vocal and zealous of the American dancer's admirers. With *sous* rashly subtracted from their meager allowances they would buy flowers at the dawn flowermarket in Les Halles, later to toss them at their idol's feet. In happy, noisy bands they would mob the stage doors of the Châtelet or the Gaité theaters, where Lugné-Poé, later to become famous as an actor-manager at the Théâtre de L'Œuvre but then acting as manager for Isadora, would finally say: "*Vous, les étudiants, vous pouvez entrer.*" And often, according to my informant, when the announced program had terminated, Isadora would step to the front of the stage and say in her quaintly accented French: "*Je vais danser encore une danse pour mes amis, les étudiants des Beaux-Arts,*" embracing in that appellation all the enthusiastic spectators of the upper balconies.

As is customary among French art students, most of these budding artists brought their sketch books to the theater and found in the dancer a much more inspiring model than the professional and official ones whose commonplace, static poses they daily transferred to paper and canvas, or modeled in clay, in the drafty *ateliers* of the state school.

José Clara was one of that enraptured band of devotees of Isadora Duncan, and for more than two decades afterwards he continued to set down his linear impressions of the dancer's various creations. When in 1913 Fate's first foul blow struck the artist and it was thought that she might never again appear in public, Clara published some of his many drawings in a Paris art review. Accompanying the sketches he wrote a brief description of the impact which Isadora made upon her audiences in the 1902–3 performances.

"No stage set except long, neutral curtains which disappeared up into darkness and left the imagination free play. Of music: the best.

"When she appeared we all had the feeling that God—that is to say Certainty, Simplicity, Grandeur and Harmony—that God was present.

"She awakened or recreated all the fervors of the Ideal and of Art; the finest dreams and highest visions were born and unfolded through the magic of her movements.

Pastel sketches by Maurice Denis. Paris, ca. 1910. (*L'Art Décoratif*, August, 1913)

"Never was Prayer more ardent, Victory more irresistible, Virgin purer, Graces younger, Fury more tragic, Serenity more luminous than she—Isadora."

One is reminded here of the story told of Emerson and Margaret Fuller who had gone to see Fanny Ellsler during her tour of America in the 1840's. "Margaret," said the poet-philosopher, "this is poetry!" "Waldo," she corrected fervently, "this is religion."

Of these early appearances of Isadora before the Parisian public, another more detailed and literary account was written at the time by the dramatist, Henri Lavedan, then at the height of his fame. Like Elie Faure, the art historian, like Mario Meunier, the distinguished Hellenist, like the artists Carrière, Rodin, Bourdelle, Grandjouan, like the poet Fernand Divoire and a host of lesser figures, Lavedan could only speak of the new dancer in dithyrambic measures, piling up superlatives.

"On an empty stage, faintly lighted, unfurnished, simply and severely draped at the back and sides with a soft, blue fabric, a young woman, vital, beautiful, has been able without the aid of any artifice and without uttering a word, to hold an audience for two hours, in one of the largest theaters of Paris. She was alone, draped rather than dressed, and so simply that the tinted veils glorified rather than betrayed the vibrant yet statuesque beauty of her body. And the end of all this beauty and courage was to celebrate a Greek dance with bare feet; this she did with such spirit that she held a vast crowd alert, charmed, deeply moved and silent while the dance lasted. It was all accomplished before the most critical audience in the world by Isadora Duncan. . . .

"Imagine for yourself a woman with a body that suggests the perfection of Greek sculpture, without the slightest resemblance to the modern French figure. The proportions are so exquisite, so harmonious that one naturally relates the whole to the thought of a pedestal. . . . Straight, slender as a sapling, robust hips, with legs at once feminine and virile, bust fragile, with the shoulders of a young girl, arms charming and energetic and curving like a precious chaplet from finger to throat—the head of Athéna by Greuze. Thus to one's first astonished and enraptured gaze, Isadora appeared, without a suggestion of self-consciousness, yet slightly timid, modest but proud, her brow without a shadow and a faint smile in her eyes."

Such ecstatic praise naturally re-echoed throughout Europe and from her Parisian

Drawing in charcoal and white chalk by Maurice Denis as a study for the Champs-Elysées
theater murals. Paris, ca. 1910.

Isadora Duncan. Pen drawing by José Clara. Paris, ca. 1910.

Brush drawing by Abraham Walkowitz. New York, 1909.

triumphs Isadora danced across the continent to conquer in turn, Germany, Austria-Hungary, Russia, Greece. Everywhere she went she was fêted; her press notices as she once expressed it to me, were no mere prosaic criticisms but were poetic dithyrambs. As always, the artists, delighting in her plastic beauty, sketched her, modeled her, painted in oil and water-color, "*die göttliche, heilige Isadora*." Von Kaulbach, Schott,

49

Wash and ink drawings by Antoine Bourdelle. Paris, ca. 1916.

Bakst, Gordon Craig, are a few of the artists whose published representations of the dancer have come down to us from that first decade of the twentieth century.

Gordon Craig, then in Germany, was just beginning to evolve his theories of stagecraft and design; he was the first artist to publish in book form—or rather in large portfolio form—a series of studies of the young dancer. The very limited edition was published in Munich in 1906, the drawings having been done the year before. It was the forerunner of ten albums or books of drawings of Isadora done at various times and places, the latest being the Walkowitz pamphlet published only last year.

The second volume dedicated wholly to the dances of the American dancer was a strange collection of calligraphic sketches in pen and ink by a French artist, Jean-Paul

Théâtre des Champs-Elysées. Architecture by the brothers Perret. Sculptured reliefs by Antoine Bourdelle. Paris, 1913.

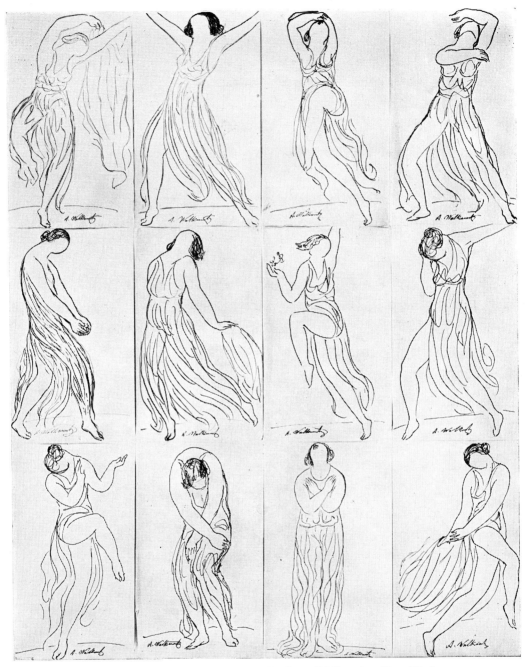

Pen and ink drawings of Isadora by Abraham Walkowitz. New York, 1920.

Lafitte. Published in the year 1910 by the then enterprising *Mercure de France*, it is notable for its preface from the pen of Elie Faure, the distinguished critic and art-historian. In part, Faure wrote:

"Yes, we wept when we saw her. It was no longer to our eyes, nor to our ears; it was no longer to our nerves that she spoke. From deep within us, when she danced, there arose a flood that swept away from the corners of our soul all the filth which had been piled up there by those who for twenty centuries had bequeathed to us their critique, their ethics, and their judgments. . . .

"When we eagerly watched her we rediscovered that primitive purity which, every two or three thousand years, reappears from the depth of the abyss of our worn-out conscience to restore a holy animality to us again. . . .

"Isadora! you have given us the certitude that the day is near when we shall once more come in fecund contact with instinctive life. You are the first flower of a tree still close to the earth and hidden among the old stripped trunks of a dying forest; but that tree will grow fiercely and scatter its seeds to make the forest thick and green again. . . ."

Faure had almost nothing to say of Lafitte's bold pen scratches. In most cases Lafitte had not cared about getting a likeness of the dancer; with a few quick strokes he sought to catch the swift movement of the limbs, the essential line of the gesture, the fall of the drapery about the body. His calligraphic scratches are a long way from the delicate yet precise line of many of the drawings made about the same time by André Dunoyer de Segonzac. To my mind that artist's line drawings are among the very finest drawings of the dance in general, or of Isadora Duncan in particular, done by any modern. They have been issued in book form in two albums, one dated 1910, the other 1913, and both are, like all the other early works about the dancer, collectors' items that are practically unobtainable.

The pastel drawings of the Frenchman, Grandjouan, also date from the same period as the Lafitte and de Segonzac ones and in their own way convey something more of the color and movement of the dancer's creations. Twenty-five of these studies were reproduced in facsimile on the same kind of colored hand-made paper originally used

Drawings in pen and ink by André Dunoyer de Segonzac. Paris, ca. 1911.

by the artist. They were bound in a very handsome hand-made album—about 48 inches by 30—of which only fifty copies were offered for sale to the public. As a contemporary advertisement in one of Isadora's programs announces: "Each album has an auto-graphed preface by Miss Duncan and is luxuriously bound in hand-tooled and hand-tinted leather. The copies are on sale at the price of 250 French francs ($50.00 at the rate of exchange then) at the author's Duncanschule at Marienhöhe, Darmstadt, and at M. Grandjouan's studio, 20 rue Poliveau, Paris."

It was during that brilliant Parisian period of the dancer's career—its apex, accord-ing to some critics—that the great sculptor, Emile-Antoine Bourdelle began to make his innumerable sketches. He first saw Isadora dance in public—apart from the Rodin fam-ily picnic in 1903—at a performance given in the Théâtre du Châtelet in 1909. From that moment on he was a devotee of the dancer and did an untold number of sketches of her, in the darkness of the theater, or at home in his *atelier*, recalling in tranquillity the divine movements which had given his sculptor's soul so much unalloyed pleasure.

In a letter dated September 10, 1912, written to Gabriel Thomas, Director of the Musée Grévin who had just been appointed to commission artists to decorate the new Théâtre des Champs-Elysées, then being constructed by the Perret brothers, Bourdelle recalls the occasion and says:

"To me it seemed that there, through her, was animated an ineffable frieze wherein divine frescoes slowly became human realities. Each leap, each attitude of the great artist remains in lightning flashes in my memory."

Later, at some soirée he saw Isadora again; she danced with the phenomenal star of the Ballets Russes—Nijinsky. In Bourdelle's private papers, notes of this evening were found.

"It seemed to me in my mind, as I watched Madame Isadora Duncan sitting or reclin-ing, that with each of her pauses she was offering me an antique marble throbbing with eternity. . . .

"I thought as I watched you: Phidias is working there.

"When you danced there was no break; it was like the seasons that follow one after the other in due course. . . .

Chalk drawing by Grandjouan. Paris, ca. 1924. Pencil sketch by John Sloan. New York, ca. 1915. (The *Masses*, 1915)

"Miss Duncan was like an eternal priestess; evoking all the masterpieces of the noblest and highest antiquity, suscitating all the masterpieces to come and that through her superbly human heart."

Later, in 1913, Bourdelle again wrote:

"When the great Isadora Duncan danced before me, thirty years of my life looking at all the great human masterpieces became suddenly animated in these planes ordained from within by the spirit's aspiration."

As for Nijinsky, this is how the sculptor saw him:

"Nijinsky is filled with the dark effluvium of free animals. He is abrupt, but naïvely more than human, and he has something of the sacred animal."

When Bourdelle began to think about his bas-relief, "The Dance," for the façade of the Théâtre des Champs-Elysées, he noted down his first conception:

"The Dance is perhaps pretty, but it is also grave. It is like a meditation, at least I would like it to be so.

"Isadora, bending and throwing back her fine head, closes her eyes to dance within in her pure emotion.

"Her hands lightly touch the marble sky. They seem to die and their life pass away in well-arranged planes.

"He, the dancer, a Nijinsky, tears himself away with a wild leap from the marble still holding him fast. His bony feet are lifted far from the earth but the block will retain this man who carries within him the winged genius of the birds."

Speaking to some of his students long after the famous theater was built and decorated, Bourdelle said:

"All my muses in the theater are movements seized during Isadora's flight; she was my principal source.

"And all of you will have recognized Isadora Duncan who soars in my frieze beside the pensive Apollo whose lyre dictated her marvelous dance to her.

"With the nine different visages which I have been able to seize from many women's faces, it is still she, Isadora, who in my frieze clashes with Isadora, in the frenzy of the hymn or the surrender of the offering."

Thus it is that the Théâtre des Champs-Elysées—one of the most beautiful in the world—is in part a great monument to Isadora. For not only is she ever-present in all Bourdelle's work, in the bas-reliefs of the marble façade of the building; but within, her movements and the very folds of her tunic appear variously in many of the frescoes which decorate the entrance hall and the corridors. In the great circular auditorium itself she looks down in many different guises from the 16 meter panel "The Dance" above the stage and also from its 13 meter companion piece "The Symphony," two of the four great murals which Maurice Denis painted. Her influence is also there in the gilded bas-relief panel "The Dance," also by Maurice Denis, which shows six of her child dancers. She is there, too, on the decorative curtain, "Fête Dionysiaque," the

Pen drawing by José Clara. Paris,
ca. 1910.

Pen drawing from memory
by Robert Henri. New
York, ca. 1916.

work of K. X. Roussel, which hangs in the smaller Théâtre de la Comédie that adjoins
the larger auditorium.

As has already been said, Bourdelle drew, both from life and from memory, innumerable sketches of Isadora. It was his intention at one time, I believe, to gather some of
them into book form. Many of them had already been published in periodicals but a
large group of the best, probably those selected for the proposed book, were left one
day in a tramway by the absent-minded sculptor and were never recovered again. An
essay by Elie Faure published in "La Revue de la Femme," in 1927 was probably intended, I should imagine from a certain indication in the text, as a preface to this volume. Faure's previous preface for the Lafitte studies published in 1910 has already been
mentioned. His later piece, not only because of the author's increased eminence as an
art historian and writer on esthetics, but because of his evaluation of the dancer and

the sculptor's work, warrants being reprinted to the extent that space allows. I have therefore made the translation which follows:

"I have never experienced a livelier emotion than on the day when I saw Isadora dance for the first time. It increased the second time, perhaps, and was renewed the third. But after that it decreased each time. For I am forced to say, having written long ago a dithyrambic piece about her, that I no longer think of her today (1927) as I thought of her during the first days of the revelation.

"I came—quickly enough—to find that art didactic, wholly cultural, expressing only an interior life subtly set forth. It exhibited ideas, even principles, more than it expressed feeling or passions. It showed more knowledge than genius, more will than rapture, and less living harmonies than 'plastic equivalences.' Isadora demonstrated while dancing. In turn she indicated in an absolutely perfect way the Bacchante and the Suppliant, the Justiciary and the Warrior, the Virgin and the Seducer, and everything that might be most definite and fully defined. I confess that the slightest Spanish dancer, thin, nervous, black as a dried olive, has more spiritual flame in her convulsive little finger than ever had that great body, sculptural as ever female body could be. The American dancer had studied dancing on the flanks of vases. But the Ronda dancer carried the dance in her own flanks. One had the unlimited sense of voluptuousness, death and universal vanity; the other had the exact sense of the art.

"I had come to think this of the great artist. But before the atrocious fate which tried to make her an ill-starred woman, I revised my judgment. . . . Pity made me more just. She conquered, by the silent command of my heart, the protest of my mind—which I had thought steadfast—against the glory that shone about the astonishing creature. I had wished to see a virtuoso in the dancer. I discovered an animator in the woman.

"It is she whom I discover in the stubborn mask drawn by Bourdelle. She created an immense movement. In the wake of the illusions she scattered like a sower, she caused to sprout in the souls of poets, dancers, sculptors, painters, and in the anonymous masses, so many emotions that are not visible but echo from place to place, creating a state of collective sensibility where the seed grows effortlessly. She rehabilitated the dance, forgotten or unknown, the humble and glorious dance, guardian, with song and popular pottery, of the concrete genius of races, ceaselessly deformed and slandered by professional artists. It was she who, in the West, preceded the triumphal entry of the Russian dancers. It was she who opened the way to the secret passages which unite by so many interwoven undulations, music and plastic art. It was she who prepared the way for the enthronement of rhythm alone, as a permanent factor of esthetic mystery, on the ruins of naturalism, academicism, romanticism, classicism, and in general of all the schools which, above everything else, attempt to represent the object. Without doubt she helped the nascent cinema to discover its real sense outside the theater, outside the imitation of forms, in that single silent empire of rhythm where dancing, painting, sculpture, and music confusedly meet.

"This great esthetic drama which washes over us and toward which, more than anyone else, Isadora has impelled us, none has lived it better than Bourdelle with his double genius wherein the most spontaneous symbolism that ever was in sculpture is locked in an ardent embrace with the sensual and realistic craft of the most accomplished of craftsmen. Two faculties which often in him express the most heartrending of the tragedies of the intelligence, that flow one over the other or join in an endless struggle where one downs the other; at other times impetuously mounting together to twist, in a single sheaf, the fuel and the fire."

Thus far I have only spoken of the European artists who drew, painted, and modeled Isadora Duncan. And that because chronologically they come before the American artists; also, in quality and quantity their work is often far superior to that done by the dancer's compatriots. Isadora, however, was not ignored by the artists of America, nor did her dance go unappreciated or unlimned.

One of her earliest admirers was the eminent Chicago sculptor, Lorado Taft. To him she was, he said: "Poetry personified. She is not the Tenth Muse but all the Nine Muses in one—and painting and sculpture as well."

Robert Henri was also among the first and most articulate of her admirers among the band of artists who acclaimed her upon her first American tour after her European triumphs. He spoke of her as "perhaps one of the greatest masters of gesture the world has

60

Crayon drawing by Van Deering Perrine,
ca. 1920. (Used as a program cover for Isadora's Russian tour of 1921.)

ever seen." She "carries us through a universe in a single movement of her body. Her hand alone held aloft becomes a shape of infinite significance." "Isadora Duncan," he said again, "dances and fills the universe. She exceeds all ordinary measure."

Another artist of the period who did many and, according to those who remember them, superb drawings of the dancer, was the painter Arthur B. Davies. Unfortunately they were all destroyed in a fire which occurred in the artist's studio. Luckier than Davies has been the painter, Abraham Walkowitz. He also, dating from that period, made an uncountable number of sketches of his favorite dancer. But he has seen to it that they have been placed in the safekeeping of such sure custodians as the print departments of museums and libraries.

Last year Walkowitz crowded together a vast collection of these sketches into an over-size pamphlet, which despite the laudable intentions of the artist, cannot be said to stand up alongside the European publications. Whatever the merits of the drawings—and some of Walkowitz's first drawings were done with obvious emotional fire and technical surety—the lack of typographical taste with which they are set forth in this pamphlet takes away much of their value.

Drawings by two American artists were especial favorites of Isadora. One chalk drawing by Van Deering Perrine she used on the cover of her programs at the Century Theatre in New York during the Spring season in 1915, at the Metropolitan Opera House in 1916, and several times in Russia. A pen and ink drawing of "Les Funerailles" by Ruth Reeves—one of a series done during the 1920 season at the Théâtre des Champs-Elysées—was used as a program cover during a *tournée* in Belgium and Holland a few years later.

Mention should surely be made here of the photographic studies of Isadora Duncan made by two Americans and unsurpassed by any others made abroad. Arnold Genthe's many studies of the dancer and her creations—some of these were published in book form in 1928—and the Acropolis series done by Edward Steichen, are not at all dwarfed in the presence of works in other pictorial mediums done by some of the world's greatest artists. Both Genthe and Steichen have raised photography, to quote the former, "from the mechanical lifeless medium it had become, to the dignity and status of a real art."

In looking over the diverse studies of the dancer done at various periods by these two Americans, one can only regret that neither photographer ever had the necessary equipment or the foresight to film at least one of the dance creations of Isadora—the ineffable little waltz, say, to the music of Brahms (Op. 39), or the mighty and tragic *Marche Slave* of Chaikovsky. As the poet Shaemas O'Sheel has said: "A few reels of film, by which the presence, the rhythm, the grace, the imperious gesture of Isadora could be evoked at will, immediate and mobile—what a treasure they would be!"

Since that treasure has been denied us we must be content with what has been bequeathed to us by Rodin and Bourdelle and de Segonzac and Clara and the happy host of great men who saw her, and had the ready wit and pictorial talent to set down for future generations some of the beauty and the magic of the Daughter of Dionysus, Isadora Duncan.

STUDIO ISADORA DUNCAN
343, PROMENADE DES ANGLAIS — NICE

— MARDI 14 SEPTEMBRE 1926 A 5 HEURES —

RECITAL JEAN COCTEAU
AVEC LE CONCOURS D'ISADORA DUNCAN
DE L'AUTEUR ET DE MARCEL HERRAND

Program cover for public recital. Pen drawing by Jean Cocteau. Nice, 1926.

Isadora Duncan: Studies for Six Dance Movements

BY GORDON CRAIG

PROLOGUE

Much noise and deep restlessness
Grief and disharmony
Is this the whole end of it?
The truth of it all?
Is it so certain then that this life
Consists only of fourfold nonsense?
Is it not far more true that this life
Is exactly the reverse,
Rest—joy and harmony,
Rhythm, the most certain truth—
And the expression of all this—Art?
Is evil then, and ugliness,
Really the image of force?
Must restlessness be the symbol of life—
Must a noisy, trying gloom spread
Over the enchantment of things—
If these are questions, I do not ask questions—
For I have no doubts at all,—

I see calmness and beauty, the strong and sweet
Draw near in a perfect manner—
Everything gives place to the spirit,
Nothing can hinder it—
Three lines or three hundred
Give the same picture—
One tone or a staff of tones
The same melody
One step or a hundred steps
Create the same dance.
Something set down—
As a record—
Something uttered on the divine theme,
Which is so simple and only simple to comprehend—
The theme which commences
"I am happy. . . . "
And ends with
". . . how fair."
This is what she dances—
Never yet has she shown dark or unbearable sorrow—
Always sunshine's around her—
Even the little shadows disappear
And flee, when she passes—
This is the real force—
She springs from the Great Race—
From the Great Companions—
From the line of Sovereigns, who
Maintain the world and make it move,
From the Courageous Giants,
The Guardians of Beauty—
The Solvers of all Riddles.

Leipzig, 1906
Translated by George Amberg

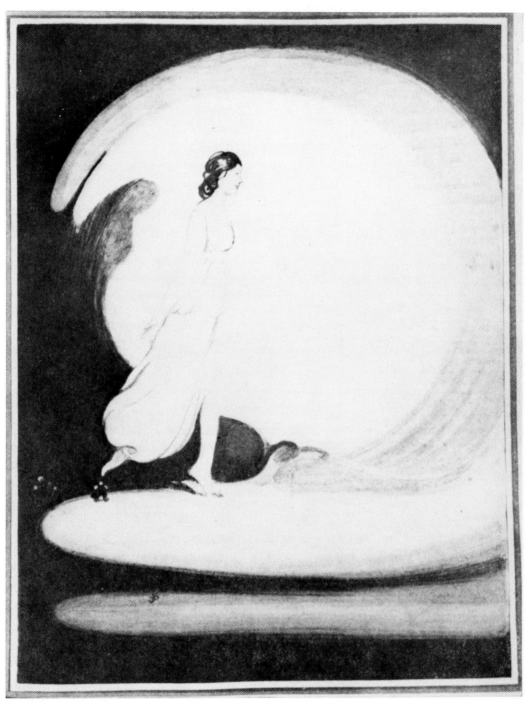

STRAUSS

66

PERI

CHOPIN

68

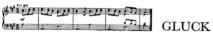

GLUCK

BEETHOVEN

69

Pastel drawing of Isadora by Gordon Craig, ca. 1904. (Courtesy George Chaffee collection)

CHRONOLOGY

1878   Born San Francisco, May 27.

1890   Danced in Augustin Duncan's San Francisco Barn Theater.

1892–4 Gave dancing lessons in San Francisco.

1896   Left for Chicago. Danced for theater managers and then in a roof garden under an assumed name.

1896   Met Augustin Daly in Chicago. He engaged her to dance in *Midsummer Night's Dream*, New York.

1896   Concerts in the Carnegie Hall Studio with Ethelbert Nevin.

1899   To London on cattle boat under the assumed name of O'Gorman.
         British Museum visits. Read Winckelman's *Journey to Athens;* sketched Greek vases.
         Danced in private homes.
         Met Andrew Lang, translator of Homer, and G. G. Watts.

1900   First visit to Paris. Visited Rodin Pavilion at the International Exposition of 1900.
         Daily visits to the Louvre. Victory of Samothrace; Venus de Milo.
         Danced in the studio of the Princess de Polignac.
         Visited Rodin's studio.

1902   First visits to Leipzig and Munich. Saw Loie Fuller dance.

1903   *First contract to dance* in a public theater. Thirty nights, Urania Theater, Budapest. Great success.

1904   Debut at Kroll Opera House, Berlin.
         First visits to Italy and Greece; plans to settle in Athens.

1905   In Vienna to present the choruses of *The Suppliants* of Aeschylus with Greek boy's chorus.
         Left Berlin for St. Petersburg.
         Saw the ballerina Mathilde Kschesinskya and admired her. Met Diaghilev, Bakst, Benois, Stanislavsky. Visited the Imperial Ballet School. Visited Moscow.
         Returned to Berlin. Opened a school in Grunewald with her sister Elizabeth.
         Met Gordon Craig, the great stage designer, in Berlin.

1906   To the Scandinavian countries. Not impressed by the Gymnastic Studio at Stockholm.
         Her first child by Craig born in Holland.
         To Florence: saw Duse in Craig's production of Ibsen's *Rosmersholm*.

1907   Toured Russia.

1908   London.

        To New York. Danced Gluck's *Iphigenia,* August, 1908.

        Met George Grey Barnard, Belasco, the painters Robert Henri and George Bellows, the poet Max Eastman.

        Danced with Walter Damrosch and Symphony Orchestra before continental tour, December, 1908, Metropolitan Opera House.

1909   Returned to Paris.

        Under direction of Lugné-Poe gave a series of successful concerts in Paris.

        Met Paris Singer.

1911   Returned to America. Danced with Damrosch Symphony.

1912   Met d'Annunzio in Paris, 1912.

1913   Her children drowned in France.

1914   Began her school at Bellevue, outside Paris; presented her pupils at the Trocadéro in June, 1914.

1915   Returned to New York. Rented studio at Fourth Avenue and 23rd Street.

        Improvised *La Marseillaise* at the Metropolitan Opera House.

        Left the United States for Naples.

1916   Sailed for South American tour.

        Returned to New York to give performances at the Metropolitan.

1917   Returned to California after twenty-two years.

1918   Returned to Paris.

1920   Revisited Athens with the hope of creating a school again.

1921   Received an invitation from the Soviet government to establish a school of dancing in Moscow.

1922   Married the Russian poet, Serge Essenin, May 3.

        Visited Elizabeth Duncan's school at Potsdam.

        Danced at the Théâtre de la Monnaie in Brussels.

        Arrived in France, the first Soviet citizen to enter.

        Came to New York with her husband and was detained at Ellis Island.

        Gave three sell-out concerts at Carnegie Hall; performances in Boston and Indianapolis.

1923   Returned to France in February.

1924   Arrived in Moscow with Essenin.

1927   Returned to Paris and gave last concert at the Théâtre Mogador, July 8.

        Killed at Nice, September 14.

BIBLIOGRAPHY OF ISADORA DUNCAN

A LIST OF REFERENCES IN AMERICAN LIBRARIES

ADAMS, MILDRED. Isadora Duncan: rhythmic way to beauty. *In* Women citizen mag. 11:26–27. New York, Oct., 1926.

The ART of Isadora Duncan. *In* Review of reviews. 63:407. London, May, 1921.

The ART of the dance. Isadora Duncan. Edited with an introduction by Sheldon Cheney. New York, Theatre Arts, Inc. 1928. 147 pages. illus. (Essays on the dance of Isadora by Max Eastman, Eva LeGallienne, Robert Edmond Jones, and others.)

ATTEMPT to awaken an art that has slept for two thousand years. *In* Current literature. Vol. 45:556–558. New York, Nov., 1908. (On the dance of Isadora Duncan.)

BEINSTOCK, J. W. Isadora's Russian husband. *In* Living age. 333:925–928. Boston, Nov., 1927.

BENGOECHA, HERNAN DE. Isadora Duncan. *In* Revista de America. 2:113–121. Paris, 1913.

BOLITHO, WILLIAM. Isadora Duncan. *In his* Twelve against the gods. . . . New York, Simon & Schuster, 1929. pp. 302–327.

BYRONIANAS, AGNES. Como conoci i Isadora Duncan. *In* Revista de revistas. pp. 20–24. April 20, 1930.

CAFFIN, CHARLES H. Henri Matisse and Isadora Duncan. *In* Camera work. 25:17–20. New York, 1929.

CLARA Y AYRATS, JOSE. Isadora Duncan; soixante-douze planches par José Clara, avec une présentation de George A. Denis. Paris, Editions Reider, 1928. 9 pages, plates.

——. Isadora Duncan. *In* L'Art décoratif. 15:103–108. illus. Paris, 1913.

CLASSIC dances of Isadora Duncan. *In* Green book album. 1:137–140. Chicago, Jan., 1909.

CORTISSOZ, ROYAL. Isadora Duncan. Reflections apropos of her work. *In* New music review. 8:201–204. New York, Mar., 1909.

CRAIG, EDWARD GORDON. Isadora Duncan. Sechs bewegungstudien, 1906. Leipzig, Inselverlag, 1906.

DELL, FLOYD. Olive Schreiner and Isadora Duncan. *In his* Women as world builders. Chicago, Forbes, 1913. pp. 41–51.

DER LING, PRINCESS. A pupil of Isadora. *In* Mentor. 22:18–20, 61. illus. New York, Sept., 1930.

DESTI, MARY. Isadora Duncan's end. London, V. Gollancz, 1929. 351 pages. illus.

——. The untold story, the life of Isadora Duncan, 1921–1927. New York, Liveright, 1929. 281 pages. illus.

DIVOIRE, FERNAND. La revolution d'Isadora Duncan. *In* Les spectacles A travers les ages. Paris, 1932. pp. 215–234. illus.

——. Isadora Duncan: Obituaire. *In* L'Illustration. 85:317. Paris, Sept. 24, 1927.

——. Isadora Duncan, fille de Promethée . . . decorées par E. A. Bourdelle. Paris Editions des muses Françaises, 1919. 58 pages. illus.

DOWD, HAROLD. The art of Isadora Duncan. *In* Theatre guild mag. 6:51–52. New York, Feb., 1929.

DUMESNIL, MAURICE. An amazing journey. Isadora Duncan in South America. New York, Ives Washburn, 1932. 311 pages. illus.

DUNCAN, IRMA. The technique of Isadora Duncan. New York, Kamin publishers, 1937. 35 pp. illus. facsim.

DUNCAN, IRMA, and MACDOUGALL, A. R. Isadora Duncan's Russian days and her last years in France, by Irma Duncan and Alice R. Macdougall. New York, Covici-Friede, 1929. 371 pp. illus.

DUNCAN, ISADORA. My life. New York, Liveright, 1927. 359 pp. illus.

——. Ma vie par Isadora Duncan. Traduit de l'anglais par Jean Allery. Paris, Librarie Gallimard, 1928. 382 pages. (My life: French text.)

——. Isadora Duncan. Memoriem. Mit 137 Abbildungen. Nach den englischen manuskript bearbeitet von C. Zell. Zurich, etc., Amalthea-verlag, 1928. 410 pp. illus. (My life: German text.)

——. . . . Mana dzive, tulkojis R. Deisons. Riga: "Gramatu draugs" 1934. 280 pp. plats. (My life: Lettish text.)

——. Moya shizn'. Perevod Ya. Yakovleva. Moskva:izdat., "Federatziya," 1930. xi–298 pp. (My life: Russian text.)

——. Mémoires d'Isadora Duncan Amour, musique et danse. *In* La revue musicale. 9:97–116. Paris, Mar., 1928. illus.

——. The dance. Introduction by Mary Fanton Roberts. *In* Touchstone mag. 2:3–16. New York, Oct., 1917.

——. The dance in relation to tragedy. *In* Theatre arts monthly. 11:755–761. New York, Oct., 1927.

——. Dancing in relation to religion and love. *In* Theatre arts monthly. 9:584–593. New York, Aug., 1927.

——. Der Tanz der zukunft (The dance of the future), eine vorlesung; übersetz und eingeleitet von Karl Federn. Leipzig, E. Diedrichs, 1930. 46 pp.

——. The dance. Authorized edition. New York, The Forest press, 1909. 28 pp. illus.

The DUNCAN dancers from Moscow. *In* Literary digest. 100:23. New York, Jan. 19, 1929.

EASTMAN, MAX. Isadora Duncan is dead. *In* Nation. 125:309. New York, Sept., 1927.

ECRITS sur la danse. Manuscripts inédits et textes communiqués par, Ch. Dallies, Fernand Divoire, Mario Menuier, Georges Delaquys, et illustrées de dessins in édits par A. Bourdelle, José Clara et Grandjouan. Paris, Grenier, 1927. 85 pp. illus.

ETSCHER, GASPARD. The renaissance of the dance. Isadora Duncan. *In* Forum mag. 46:322–329. Sept., 1911.

EVAN, BLANCHE. Isadora Duncan. Road to the dance. *In* Theatre arts monthly. 19:27–34. New York, Jan., 1935.

FORD, J. E. Isadora Duncan. *In* Putnam's mag. 5:481. New York, Jan., 1909. (A poem.)

FREEMAN, HELEN. Isadora. *In* Theatre arts monthly. 11:942. New York, Dec., 1927. (A poem.)

FREJAVILLE, G. Isadora Duncan. *In* Jour. des débats politiques et litteraires. 34:531–532. Paris, Sept. 23, 1927.

GOLD, MICHAEL. The loves of Isadora. *In* New masses. 4:20–21. New York, Mar., 1929.

HOWARD, RUTH ELEANOR. Isadora Duncan "In Memoriam." *In* American dancer. Los Angeles, Oct., 1927. pp. 11, 30. port.

ISADORA Duncan's Art. *In* Literary digest. 50:1018–1019. New York, May, 1915.

——. *In* Outlook. 147:103–104. New York, Sept. 28, 1927.

ISADORA Duncan's artistic credo. *In* Literary digest. 95:28–29. New York, Oct. 8, 1927.

ISADORA Duncan dancers. *In* Le Théâtre et Comoedia Illustré. Paris, Feb., 1922, no. 2, p. 141. (A note on the concert of Anna, Lisa and Erica Duncan, with illustrations.)

——. *In* Le Théâtre et Comoedia Illustré. 2:141. Paris, Feb., 1922.

ISADORA Duncan dances the Marseillaise. *In* Current opinion. 62:31. New York, Jan., 1917.

ISADORA Duncan's triumphs and tragedies. *In* Literary digest. 95:48–52. New York, Oct., 1927.

ISADORA Duncan's Moscow school. *In* Le Théâtre et Comoedia Illustré. 39:649–652. Paris, Nov., 1924.

ISADORA Duncan. *In* Comoedia Illustré. pp. 122–123. Paris, Feb., 1909. (A note on her concert.)

——. *In* Comoedia Illustré. 3:269. Paris, Feb., 1911. (A note on her concert at the Châtelet.)

——. *In* The Theatre . . . 8:324. New York, Dec., 1908. (A poem to Isadora by Charles H. Towne.)

——. *In* The Theatre. 3:184. New York, Aug., 1903. port.

——. *In* The Theatre. 14:122. New York, Oct., 1911. (A poem to Isadora.)

——. *In* Comoedia Illustré. 4:321. Paris, Feb., 1912.

——. Obituary. *In* Theatre arts monthly. 11:842–843. New York, Nov., 1927.

ISADORA Duncan and Pavlova. *In* Harper's weekly. 58:5. New York, Nov. 29, 1913.

ISADORA Duncan: dessins de Albertine Bernouard, René Piot et Louis Sue; hors-texte de Antoine Bourdelle, José Clara et Grandjouan. Paris, G. Labruyere, 19—.

——. An episode in her career. *In* Harper's mag. 158:246–249. New York, Jan., 1929.

KAYE, JOSEPH. The last chapters of Isadora's life. *In* Dance mag. 12:21–24; 30–33; 36–39. New York, April–July, 1929.

KINEL, LOLA. This is my affair . . . Boston, Little, Brown, 1937. xxv–335 pp. illus. (Autobiography of Isadora Duncan's secretary.)

LAFITTE, JEAN-PAUL. Les danses d'Isadore Duncan; avec une préface de Elie Faure. Paris, Mercure de France, 1910. 14 pp. 36 plates.

LALOY, LOUIS. Isadora Duncan et la danse nouvelle. *In* La revue musicale. 4:249–253. Paris, May, 1904.

LEVEIN, SONYA. The art of Isadora Duncan. *In* Metropolitan mag. 42:38–39. New York, June, 1915.

LEVINSON, ANDRE. Isadora Duncan. *In his* La danse d'aujourd'hui . . . Paris, Editions Duchartre et Van Buggenhoudt, 1929. pp. 142–161.

LUGNE-POE. Isadora Duncan . . . et nos Oeuvriers. *In* Revue politique et litteraire. 71:3–8. Paris, Jan., 1933.

LUHAN, MABEL DODGE. Isadora Duncan—Elizabeth Duncan—The Elizabeth Duncan school. *In her* Movers and shakers. New York, Harcourt, Brace, 1936. pp. 319–348.

——. Isadora Duncan. *In* New English weekly. pp. 396–399. London, Aug. 11, 1932.

MacDONALD, CLAIRE. Isadora Duncan. *In* Home and abroad. 8:124–126. London, Spring, 1929.

MACDOUGALL, A. R. Dancer speaks. *In* Touchstone mag. 8:336–339. New York, Feb., 1921. (A note on Isadora.)

MARSH, LUCILE. The shadow of Wigman in the light of Duncan. *In* Dance mag. pp. 12–13, 62. New York, May, 1931.

MASON, ARTHUR. Mistress of the dance. *In* Green book album. 1:137–140. Chicago, Jan., 1909.

MEEUS, MARIE-LOUISE DE. A star danced: Isadora Duncan and Anna Pavlova. *In* Cornhill mag. 72:544–551. London, May, 1932.

MESTRE, JULIA. Isadora Duncan. *In* Revista de la facultad de letras y ciencias. 30:385–395. Havana, 1921.

MILLE, PIERRE. Isadora Duncan. *In* Le Théâtre. 244:20–21. Paris, Feb., 1909. illus.

MISS Isadora Duncan en haar school te Gruenwald bij Berlin. *In* Elsevier's Geillus. maandschrift. 32:88–102. Amsterdam, 1906.

MISS Isadora Duncan's matinees at the Prince of Wales Theatre, London. *In* Spectator. 126: 524–525. London, April 23, 1921.

NEWMAN, ERNEST. Dances of Isadora Duncan. *In* Living age. 309:606–607. Boston, June, 1921.

MONROE, HARRIET. Isadora Duncan: Golden moments. *In* Poetry mag. 31:206–207. New York, Jan., 1928.

NORMAN, GERTRUDE. Appreciation of Isadora Duncan. *In* The Theatre. 5:36–39. New York, Feb., 1905.

O'SHEEL, SHAEMUS. Isadora Duncan, priestess. *In* Poet lore. 21:480–492. Boston, Nov., 1910.

PARKER, H. T. Isolated Isadora. *In his* Eight notes; voices and figures of music and the dance. New York, Dodd, Mead, 1922. pp. 231–238.

PAVLOVA, NELIA. Essenine et Isadora Duncan. *In* Revue mondiale. pp. 63–66. Paris, Jan., 1930.

PICKERING, RUTH. Isadora Duncan. *In* Nation. 128:202–204. New York, Feb., 1929.

ROBERTS, MARY FANTON. The dance of the future as created and illustrated by Isadora Duncan. *In* Craftsman mag. 13:48–56. New York, Oct., 1908. illus.

——. France honors Isadora Duncan and helps her to establish a free school of dancing. *In* Touchstone mag. 7:303–309. New York, July, 1920.

RUHL, ARTHUR. Some ladies who dance. *In* Collier's mag. 44:17–18. New York, Feb., 1910.

A RUSSIAN's opinion of Isadora Duncan. *In* Living age. 323:401–402. Boston, Nov. 15, 1924.

SAURET, HENRIETTE. Isadora Duncan, impératrice errante. *In* Revue mondiale. pp. 161–172. Paris, Mar., 1928.

SCHREIBER, GERHARDT. Arthur Nikisch und Isadora Duncan. *In* Der Tanz. pp. 22–23. Berlin, May, 1929.

SECHAN, LOUIS. Isadora Duncan. *In his* La danse grecque antique . . . Paris, E. de Boccan, 1930. pp. 315–357.

SELDES, GEORGE. What love meant to Isadora. *In* Mentor mag. 18:25–27; 64–65. Springfield, Ohio, Feb., 1930.

SERGINES. Les Echos: Isadora Duncan. *In* Annales politiques et litteraires. 89:322. Paris, Oct. 1, 1927.

STOKES, SEWELL. Isadora Duncan; an intimate portrait. London, Brentano, 1928. 208 pp. illus.

SVETLOV, VALERIEN. Duncan. *In his* Le ballet contemporain . . . St. Petersburg, 1912. pp. 61–84.

To Isadora Duncan: a tribute from a young student. *In* Touchstone mag. 7:307–308. New York, July, 1920.

VAN VECHTEN, CARL. The new Isadora. *In his* Merry-go-round . . . New York, A. Knopf, 1918. pp. 307–317.

WERNER, MORRIS R. Isadora Duncan. *In his* To whom it may concern. New York, Cape & Smith, 1931. pp. 245-277.

YORSKA, MME. Isadora Duncan. What she hopes to achieve in the future. *In* Arts and decoration. 27:46, 80. New York, Aug., 1927.

YOUNG, STARK. Isadora Duncan. *In* New republic. 57:43-44. New York, Nov. 28, 1928.

Bookplate monogram (I. D.).

Woodcut by Gordon Craig, ca. 1906.

ALBUMS AND BOOKS OF DRAWINGS OF ISADORA DUNCAN

ALGI, VAN SAANEN. Isadora Duncan. A book of line drawings. Paris. 1920(?).

BOURDELLE, EMILE-ANTOINE. Isadora Duncan, Fille de Promethée. Water-color and line drawings with poems by Fernand Divoire. Les Muses Françaises. Paris. 1919.

CLARA, JOSÉ. Isadora Duncan.* An album of 72 plates. Drawings in water-color and line. Preface in French by Georges Denis. Reider. Paris. 1928.

CRAIG, EDWARD GORDON. Sechs Bebegungstudien.* An album of six lithographic drawings, each matter and loose. Prologue in German. Limited Edition. Leipzig. 1906.

DE SEGONZAC, ANDRE DUNOYER. Dessins sur les danses d'Isadora Duncan précédés de La Danseuse de Diane. Line drawings. (Preface in French by Fernand Divoire.) Limited Edition. La Belle Edition. Paris. 1910.

——. XXX Dessins:* Line drawings of Isadora alone and with her child dancers. (Also a few of Ida Rubinstein, and some studies of boxers.) Limited Edition. Les Editions du Temps Present. Paris. 1913.

GRANDJOUAN. A series of 25 colored pastel facsimiles on colored, hand-made paper. Paris. 1913(?).

JACQUES, LUCIEN. Isadora Duncan. A book of line drawings. Paris. 1920(?).

LAFITTE, JEAN-PAUL. Les Danses d'Isadora Duncan. A book of line drawings. 38 Plates. In four sections: The Religious Dances; The Vases; The Bacchantes; The Return of the Warriors. Preface in French by Elie Faure. Mercure de France. 1910.

WALKOWITZ, ABRAHAM. Isadora Duncan in her Dance.* Pamphlet of water-color and line drawings. Forewords by Mary Fanton Roberts, Maria-Theresa, Carl Van Vechten, Arnold Genthe and Shaemus O'Sheel. Haldeman-Julius. Kansas City, 1945.

PHOTOGRAPHS

GENTHE, ARNOLD. 24 Photographic studies of Isadora Duncan.* Foreword by Max Eastman. Mitchel Kennerly. New York and London. 1929.

* In the Department of Dance and Theatre Design, Museum of Modern Art, New York City.

Isadora as a member of the Augustin Daly Theatrical Company. New York, 1896.

Portrait study of Isadora Duncan.
Paris, ca. 1900.

Chicago, ca. 1896.

Portrait study. Munich, 1903.

New York, 1922.

Portrait study by Arnold Genthe. New York, 1916.

Isadora's studio in Moscow. Moscow, 1924.

Isadora Duncan and her companion (Mary Desti) in the car in which she was killed. Taken the day before her death. From a snapshot owned by Martha Graham. Photographer unknown. Nice, September 13, 1927. (Courtesy Martha Graham and Barbara Morgan)